SEXCESSFULLY PROMOTIONS

DR. ESTELLA INGRAM-LEVY

authorHOUSE®

AuthorHouse™
1663 Liberty Drive
Bloomington, IN 47403
www.authorhouse.com
Phone: 1 (800) 839-8640

Published by AuthorHouse 04/23/2018

ISBN: 978-1-5462-3801-0 (sc)
ISBN: 978-1-5462-3800-3 (e)

CONTENTS

Dedicated
to
YOU
and
...my beloved Sisters and Brothers...
All Educators
All Employees
All Employers

Special thanks to all those whose effort and co-operation enabled me to write this book

ACKNOWLEDGEMENT

Words cannot adequately express my sincere gratitude to first: to the Creator, that continues to bestow His Blessings upon me, and provided the courage for me to write this book, to help prevent future unjustifiable promotions; to my seven sisters and five brothers who have always believed in and supported me in all of my endeavors; to those individuals who shared their stories for further preventions of Sexcessfully Promotions and Sexual Harassment; to my colleagues who so unselfishly expressed their continuous support and encouragement to alert society of the wrong and inappropriate behavior in the workforce; to the teacher who lost the battle with cancer, because she refused to have sex with an executive, thus, her life became very stressful during her tenure in education; and to all mankind, you need to know that you are most certainly appreciated.

OVERVIEW

This is an extraordinary moving book. One of which that others in the workforce will be able to easily relate to and perhaps share your sexual harassment experiences. This book will help you to identify individuals in key positions, whom you may know were SexCessFully Promoted.

The theme of this book is centered around Education, (SexCessFully Promotions in the School System). The author shares stories of her 28 years experiences in Education. She never received a promotion during this tenure, because she refused to have sex with individuals in top positions, regardless of having been more then qualified. Unlike many other individuals in the school system, whereas in many cases, violated their morals, values and spiritual beliefs just to leave the the classroom, and have a title.

The author shares "true" cases that she witnessed, as well as others who were willing to openly share horrors of sexual harassment. In many cases there were some individuals who were either promoted or demoted. In one very traumatic case, the result of sexual harassment initiated the death of a classroom teacher who had refused to become sexually involved with her superior.

Although, the events in this book are ongoing, there are suggestions and solutions that one could adopt after having read this book to help prevent, and or make known this type of harassment without having to be afraid, or undergo any type of manic depression, etc.

This book is particularly about the author's strength, courage and moral that she so eloquently and honestly exemplify throughout the dialogue to help make the public aware of the continuous humiliation that one faces from individuals in decision-making positions.

Finally, this book exposes the discrimination among individuals, in reference to size, age, complexion and other.

SUMMARY

SexCessFully Promotions seem to be a way of life for unqualified individuals to obtain "key" positions in the workforce. Promotions that are SexCessFully acquired, usually result in the decline and growth of productivity. Individuals who refuse to become SexCessFully Promoted usually face major crises, inclusively, throughout their career.

PREFACE

The content of this book is based on my experiences and/or observations, and others who were willing to share their stories. The content in this book shall not imply that all promotions are, or were sexually oriented. However, it is intended to make individuals aware of society ills in reference to females and males, particularly females promotions. Hopefully, the material in this book will initiate thought processes that will be geared toward honesty, integrity, qualification, experience, and preparation for criteria-based promotions, not only sexual oriented. Although, the content of the book is NON-FICTION, it is not my intent to create any anger or discredit those individuals who were promoted, because they met all essential criteria for the specific promotion.

Unfortunately, during my 28 years in education, I have seen too many SexCessFully Promotions. The content of this book will reveal specific examples of how one received promotions. To maintain neutrality and anonymity, I will not use any generic names. Instead, I referred to females as for example, "Lady X, or Ms. X", and males as "Gentleman Y, or Mr. Y."

As you read through this book, you will find that dates have been very carefully omitted. I purposely avoided using dates to prevent the pointing of fingers to specific individuals.

In addition, by writing this book, it is my hope to create an action plan to comprehensively respond to sexual harassment challenges without having to be reprimanded, or put on the "Never Promotion List."

After you have completed reading this book, you, too, may be able to recall antagonizing experiences with your profession. I felt compelled to finally share some of mine and others stories. I am very much aware that those individuals who have been SexCessFully Promoted will not be pleased with the content of this book. Nonetheless, it is imperative that this sexual harassment be exposed to the public to prevent any more unfair treatment to particularly the younger female professionals, and to attempt to prevent further SexCessFully Promotions, and that body, size, age, or anything else will not prevent qualified individuals from receiving a promotion.

Finally, although, the major focus of employment in the content of this book is on education, as one reads through the content, I am convinced that one will be able to recognize the same experiences, and or situations in his/her place of employment and profession.

INTRODUCTION

On-going sexual harassment by the upper Epsilon is still alive among professionals, regardless to past media exposure of the "select-few" who have been appointed to top positions. Unfortunately, those professionals who have been, and still will be sexually harassed will not be afforded the opportunity to air their grief, or be given the chance to tell their story with any kind of conviction. The main reason for not airing such, and having to continue to suffer all of the psychological stresses and depression is fear. Fear serves as the umbrella as to whether one would come forward or remain silent. The composition of this fear includes very poor treatment from their present employer, labeling individuals as "trouble-makers," as well as never ever having the hope for any kind of promotions or advancement throughout their tenure of employment.

The intent of this book is to help others learn early, be more prepared for the denial of promotions, continuous rejections after interviews, and thus, to prevent losing respect in the system for receiving such abuse, while having to continue to perpetuate excellence in their performance.

The intent of this book also is to share with the public hidden sexual harassment that has been kept undercover throughout my 28 years in education. Throughout my 28 years in education, I, as well as many other teachers who refused to become sex "slaves" for various individuals at the top have never been promoted. Even though I won "Teacher of the Year" out of 12000 employees, won the Higher Educational Award, many Mayoral and Gubernatorial Awards, McDonald Adhov Educational Award, Baltimore's Woman of the Year Award, and won over 45 awards during the same year. In addition, I have made many television appearances, have done several different radio stations two-way talk shows, and have served as a facilitator for educators both nationally and internationally who wanted to learn more about how to raise Urban Students Standards who were economically and socially deprived.

By my having refused to have become SexCessFully Promoted, all of the aforementioned did not mean anything. I, along with other colleagues continued to observe others who received promotions, and were placed in top positions, who just did not exemplify the qualifications for such positions. I have seen individuals promoted, to my knowledge, who had never won anything, or even had public recognition get these type of promotions. Nonetheless, they had far less tenure then others who were qualified for such positions in the system.

It has always been that subconscious voice that continued to remind me of what the Commissioner had told me during my very early years of teaching, which was, "until you learn how to drop your panties, you will never be promoted, and life will be very difficult for you in this system, you must learn how this system works." It took all of these years of having been in education to realize that the commissioner was telling the truth. However, I do not regret, or apologize in reference to the fact that I refused to have sex to receive promotions for any titled positions.

My only regret is that I was introduced to such injustice treatment while having to live for 28 years with such overt sexual harassment, having to absorb all of the fears of making the public aware such treatment. My final regret has been the lost of respect for the system, and my observation of witnessing continuous SexCessFully Promotions.

Again, it is not my intent to infer that all promotions have been sexually oriented. However, it is my intent to share with the public my own observations, and a few others stories and comments of their having also been sexually harassed throughout the system. Although, there will be individuals who may want to challenge the content of this book for accuracy, I will be more than willing to overtly come forward and defend its content without reservations.

Included in the content of this book are somewhat oral graphical illustrations and expressions, not inclusively of just my observations and knowledge, but those of others who have been sexually harassed, and because of not having consented to go all the way, they continue to live day-by-day with rejections, depression, and many other relevant abuses. *This book will focus on both male and female who have been sexually harassed to either obtain a promotion, and or to maintain a position. Some males comments are also included in the content of this book.*

Finally, in addition, this book contains stories of individuals who tell about many disappointments, and the psychological stress of having often times to sit at the same table with the harasser, while hiding their inner feeling, and continuing to have to go along with unfair treatment. Therefore, a change must come so that SexCessFully Promotions will be exposed and prevented.

CHAPTER ONE

PREPARATION FOR THE SURPRISE

As a youngster, my wildest dreams would never have been actually witnessing SexCessfully Promotions. I was not around males figures during my very early years of life. My father died as I turned 5 years old. At this time, there were 13 children. The oldest two were in their mid-thirties from a previous marriage. It was approximately a 12 year gap between those two and my mother and father eleven. The other 11 ranged in age of two years apart, in two situations, not exactly two years. There were 8 females and 5 males. The males were mixed in between the females in reference to age. Although, throughout the years, I had been told about the philosophy of my father from the older siblings.

My father strongly believed that an education would probably be the backbone for achievement throughout one's life. This philosophy was instilled in us on a daily basis in my family. Even though, he hardly went to school at all. We do not know if he even had a third grade education, because his parents passed when he was just about 3 years old. Therefore, out of a family of 14 other siblings, a couple of the elder siblings kept him from time to time. If he were alive today his age would be approximately 105 years old.

Other detriments that my father had to face were serious segregation during his era in the state of North Carolina that would have been in any state in America during this time. After my father was married, and had the other eleven children, he was determined that his children would be exposed to any available opportunities. It was because of his lacking in education, he focused on it very religiously with his children. Never in a day, however, perhaps, any of the children would have dreamed of having acquired the education, that the bottom line would be based on SexCessFully Promotions.

In my family, the older children were responsible for teaching the younger children. Because of this philosophy, and prior to my becoming school age, I was taught the basics before my very first day of school. I knew how to tell time, the ABC's, how to count from 1-100, I even knew how to use phonics and read and write. I was familiar with high school literature and other disciplines, because those were the only books we had. This came about as the results of some teachers recognition of various exceptional skills and talents among my older siblings. When they had any type of materials, such as old torn books, magazines, newspapers that could no longer be in in the school, they gave them to my siblings. We were not economically situated to have the luxury during these years to have purchased these items. These materials were brought home, and utilized on a daily basis, for, this was the first beginning of my acquisition of knowledge and skills.

Upon entering school, which was not referred to as Kindergarten, but, we called it the Primer grade. I am still not convinced if were calling the grade Primary, all I can recall is the word, "Primer." Since all of this was new, I was very excited and anxious to become involved. So the teacher, whom I can remember, did not appear to be a real person, but a supreme being who was willing to make a miracle happen. The teacher began to do the children things as usual. I can recall, just trying to answer all the questions. It was no doubt, the teacher knew I had arrived. It was because the same teacher had taught all of my older siblings, I knew now, that she must not have been surprised with my behavior. She began the day by putting the large letters of the ABC's around the boarder of the small worn chalk board. As fast as she would place them, I was calling out loud each of them, without any invitation from her to do so. My classmates had no clue as to what was happening. Then she put several large numbers on the board, positioned them likewise underneath the alphabets. My behavior was the same. My teacher knew that she had to very quickly use diversion in her lesson to meet my needs. Therefore, she asked if I would help the other children. This made me feel exceptionally special. I was the teacher's helper throughout that first year.

The end of the year had come. I was promoted to the first grade. Most of my first grade year was serving as a tutor for the other students. Please be reminded at this point, I had been, and still was being taught at home, concepts and principles that my older siblings were learning and knew, including high school information. This year seemed to have flown by like a quick breeze. I was promoted to the second grade. I still had the same teacher, who probably was convinced by now, that other provisions for had to be considered and implemented. My stay in the second grade was very brief. My old teacher escorted me across the hall to a new teacher. Somehow, when I arrived the new teachers' class it was the third grade. I was left in her class. This did not phase me, because I did not know the difference from one grade to the other. Anyway, this did not alter or have any effect on my behavior. My aggressive behavior continued in the third grade class. Again, I became the teachers' aid, and helped with the facilitating of the lessons. This trend remained the same until I arrived to high school.

Upon entering into high school, along with maturation, I became more focused. It was time to really buckle-down and think about after high school plans. During my high school tenure, I focused on making the best grades, and maintaining perfect attendance. I focused on taking all the prerequisites and acquiring those requirements that were essential for making a smooth transition from high school to college. During my high school tenure, I participated in many extra -curricular activities. I entered and won essay contests, science fair projects, and other academic awards. Meanwhile, I never lost focus in reference to the skills needed for matriculating in college.

My high school years appeared to have gone by very quickly. As graduation approached, like most high school seniors, fear seemed to have played a major influence on my classmates behavior. Some were feeling very stressful, while others were trying to make the decisions as to seek immediate employment, or continue at a post-secondary institution.

As May came to past, we knew that graduation was upon us. Credits had already been added and checked, and the graduation candidates confirmed for the program. The announcement was made to the potential graduates, naming the highest average in the class. When my name was called as the class valedictorian, I must admit, I was not surprised. I had maintained the highest average in my class since grades 9-12.

By now, I was even more focused as to how I would make the transition from high school to college very smoothly. I had gained a lot of confidence and self-esteem. I am convinced that my seriousness, enthusiasm, ambition, and focus, were the contributors for such smooth transition.

The month of September seemed to have come very quickly. Perhaps, because of the anxiety level of entering into a new phase of my life, college. By my not having counselors in my high school, I really did not know what to expect. Although, my older siblings had finished college, and throughout my life, I was told bits and pieces about college life, but never, had faced the real challenge.

The time had come for registration. I did not know the difference between a 100 level course, and a 300 level course. So as I completed my schedule, I mixed 100 level courses with a couple of 300 courses. There were no advisors to adequately help me with this process. I recall the first day of my classes, all Professors were males, except for one female. Some of my Professors appeared very serious, while others appeared to have been there getting paid, so to speak.

Most of my Professors used the same strategy by saying, "there will be no A's or B's in this class. The author gets the A, I get the B, and there may be a couple of C's, if you are lucky." This statement did not set too well with me. After all, during my high school years from grades 9-12, I had only received three B's and all other grades were A's. I had never received a C or below grade.

The first semester was in full swing by now. I recall very distinctly and elder male Professor requesting to see me after class. At this level, a student dared to be disobedient. After class, I went to his desk. He carefully waited until all the students had left the area, and began to tell me about how I could succeed very well in his class. He told me, if I would allow him to take me out sometimes, that I would not have to worry about passing his class. I was totally shocked with his statement. Needless to mention, I did not have a clue as to what he was talking about. I thought taking out, meant either going to a movie, or going to dinner, never going to a teacher's house. I asked him (trying to get a feel), what type of movies did he like, etc. His response was that he did not go to movies. Then, I asked him about the different types of restaurants, and food he liked. He said that he usually picked up food, and took it to his residence for his guests.

By now, the picture was beginning to become clear, that I would be going to his house. At this moment, I paused, and told him that I'll have to think about it, and let him know my decision soon. He said, very abruptly, "don't wait too long, the semester will soon be over." This began to worry me. I did not know what to do at this point. I was afraid to share this with my classmates, because the implication would have been, the only way to succeed in the gentleman's class is that one must go out with him, and this would have left the impression that any sincere studying and hard work would have been in vain.

The fear kept building in me. It became extremely difficult for me to attend his class, because I knew he was waiting for my reply to his request. I knew that my morals and values would not have permitted me to have gone to his house. Finally, I had to tell someone. One afternoon, while having dinner with my family, and after having reached my saturation point behind all of this, I told my older sister that we had to about something very important that been really worrying me. After dinner, she agreed to listen. She suggested going to the basement of the house so that we could be along. She knew that this must had been very private.

I began to tell her in details about this male Professor. She became very angry. She insisted that she was going to report him to the higher authority at the university. I pleaded with her very desperately, not to do that. I was too afraid of further being reprimanded, and having to obtain the reputation of a trouble-maker, that could have been very detrimental to my tenure at the university. Needless to mention, receiving a failing grade in his class. I knew that Professors talked among themselves, and I did not want to have any of them formulating pre-meditated behavior patterns before my arrival to their class.

Back at his class, I managed to keep a very low profile. I carefully avoided any opportunity to be along, or even having to talk to this Professor. However, this did not delete the fear that I maintained while in his class during the entire semester. From time to time, he would look at me during class very cunningly. Each time that I would see him looking at me, I pretended that I was engaged in an activity, such as reading or writing something. The semester was finally over. How happy was I. I knew my grade should have been either an A or B, but, I did not challenge him. At this point, I was so pleased that the class was over, and I did not comply to his request, until the unfair grade did not matter, unfortunately.

Fortunately, I learned how to handle each case, thereafter much better after having experienced this first semester. In addition, as time passed, my classmates and I began to talk among ourselves about our experiences at the university. I began to realize that females were not the only ones who were sexually harassed. Males had, and were also harassed by male Professors who were homosexual.

I recall very distinctly one male student talking about his Professor in his Art class. He had grown up in a Northern State, and was more familiar with a variety of behavior patterns. He shared with me that his Art teacher had invited him over to his apartment for drinks. He accepted the invitation. While visiting with the Professor, the Professor gradually started discussing sex, and asked to show him his bedroom. The male student knew exactly what was on the Professor mind. The Professor told the male student, if he would become his close friend, he would guarantee an A in his class. The male student shared with me how frighten he was, and all he could think about at the moment was how to escape from his apartment.

Finally, the male student said that the Professor took off his clothes, and did not appear that he was going to take him home. The student said he pretended to have gone to the bathroom that was passed the entry to his apartment. Instead of going to the bathroom, he very quietly opened the door and left. The next class time, the Professor asked the student why did he leave, etc. The student told him that after a certain hour, he was afraid that his father would start to worry, and if he were not at home, would have contacted the police to look for hm. Therefore, and during the remaining of the class, the student said that he was treated very poorly, and his final grade was a D, regardless of the fact, that he did all required work.

After graduation, I felt very relieved that I would not have to always have the fear of wondering when the time would come of having to go through this pattern with other male Professors. Little did I know, that was a minute appetizer of things yet to come. My only regret is that I was introduced to such injustice treatment, while having to live 28 years with such overt sexual harassment, having to absorb all the fears of making the public aware of such treatment. My final regret has been the loss of respect for the system, and my observation and witnessing continuous SexCessFully Promotions.

Again, it is not my intent to infer that all promotions have been sexually oriented. However, it is my intent to share with the public my own observations and experiences, and a few others who were willing to have their story told. Although, there will be individuals who would want to challenge the content of this book for accuracy, I will be more than willing to oververtly come forward and defend the content in this book without reservations.

CHAPTER TWO

MY FIRST THREE YEARS IN EDUCATION

(Meeting the School Board Commissioner)

After having graduated from college, like most young adults, I felt very good about my accomplishments. I felt that I was well prepared, and had acquired and met various criteria for growth in education, based on qualifications, etc. I would have dared to have entertained the concepts of Sexcessfully Promotions.

My first teaching assignment was at a Junior High School. The system had not converted to Middle Schools. My dream was to really share and help students and parents with their needs. I began by participating in everything that became available to enhance my skills. Immediately, I joined the PTSA. After which, I discovered that there were school board meetings once a month, and that these meetings were opened to the public.

Reflecting back to my college years, I was fortunate to have worked three consecutive summers at the Department of Education. My experience was very unique. I performed a variety of duties, including interviewing teachers, all kind of record keeping, and learning about the total business, concepts and principles of education for the city.

Nonetheless, my first year was going by very slowly. There were no overt problems, not even disciplinarian with my classes. One day, while standing in front of my students, I felt some type of outside energy. When I looked up, I saw about ten people standing in the rear of my classroom. I did not recognize any of them. I did not know what to do. They remained silent, and kept observing. Since I had earned my Bachelors in Science, I really did not know which career path I was going to pursue. I had not concluded to teach, or take advantage of research opportunities, working in some lab, or what. During this era, opportunities were gradually opening for minorities in all disciplines, and particularly science. Therefore, the individuals in the rear of my classroom did not have a bearing on me at all. During that time, I did not think that I was interested in teaching, and making it my life career. However, I had been sent to this particular school with high recommendations by the Chair of the Science Department from the university. I was too polite to just quit, after others appeared to have been so confident with my expertise.

While the visitors were still standing in the rear of my classroom, a thought came upon me. The thought, I vividly recall, was to really act very tough, and work the students very hard, my thought was that I would get fired. I began to toughen up, and performing on a very high level with my students.

Amazingly enough, the students behavior was very affirmative to this quick change. When the bell rang, and the class was dismissed, the visitors came forward. I was hoping that they were going to tell me how wrong I was, and that my expectations and standards were too high, and in other words, would have told me that I did not fit the criteria for a teacher.

How far from the truth this thinking was on my behave. Instead of saying all of the above, everything that they said was just the opposite. They all commended me for having done such an excellent job as a new teacher. They related to me how impressed they were. They mentioned how disciplined my students were, and to my surprise, they told me that they were going to make me a model teacher for all new teachers to observe.

I must mention, the composition of the visitors were Specialists, Area Superintendents, and some Board of School Commissioners.

Among those visitors, was a male commissioner. He asked why hadn't he seen me at the School Board Meeting. I did not let on, that I did not know the School Board even met, and that the public could attend. Politely and professionally, I asked him the time, date, and place of the meetings, and promised him that would attend the next meeting, although I was reluctant to attending the board meetings alone.

After committing to attend the School Board Meetings, I began to ask different colleagues to go along with me. All of them said that they were not interested, and that such meetings would be very boring, and they would just be wasting time, because school board members did not care about teachers. Somehow, I had a problem with believing that.

The school board met the third Thursday of each month. I braced myself to take this bold step, and to attend my first School Board Meeting. Upon arriving at the place of the meeting, I did not see many automobiles. This surprised me, after all, it was my thinking that if this were where decisions were made, and information disseminated, there should have been problems trying to find a parking space. I sat in my car for a while, however, watching different ones enter into the building. I felt a bit nervous, but managed to walk into the meeting s if I knew what was happening. The meeting was called to order. At first, I was very confused because I did not know the prototype. After a while, I began to relate to how everything was focusing. The audience was composed of a few principals, parents and community leaders. I did not recognize any teachers. There were not many people in attendance. It appeared to have been approximately 25-35. I thought that my colleagues were right, and that this is definitely not for teachers. During the entire meeting, they never said a thing about the teaching staff. I began to wonder, if I had wasted my time by attending.

When the meeting adjourned, several of the attendants were very curious about who I was, and actually wanted to know my reason for attending. They knew that I was not a principal, or worked at Central Office. I told them that I was a new teacher. This, however, was a little surprising to those individuals to meet a first year teacher at a school board meeting. The people seemed to have been regulars. They all knew each other. This was confirmed by their conversations, and when they departed, they made statements in reference to seeing one another at the next month's meeting.

After the meeting was over, I did not leave immediately. I stayed until hardly anyone was left and the parking lot. I began to my car when I heard a quiet voice say, "hello Miss" referring to the school name to which I had been assigned. It was obvious that he had forgotten my name, but recalled who I was from the school. He said that he was glad that I could make it. He continued talking and walking me to my car. When I arrived at my car, and proceeded to get in, he handed one of his cards to me, and said, "call me." From my reactions, he must have interpreted my thinking at the moment, that was, why should I call you, I'm not having a problem, or I don't even know what to talk about with you. He recognized this behavior very quickly. He responded by saying, "never mind, it may be very difficult for you to reach me at the office, so I'll need your number to call you." Without hesitation or reservation, I tore a small piece of paper from the meeting agenda, and wrote my telephone number down for him. He asked what the best time to call when we could talk without being disturbed. Since I was single, I knew that it would have been difficult for me to be disturbed, not that any time would have been appropriate for him to call.

Even though I did not respond so quickly, avoiding leaving any kind of impressions that I did not have other activities going on in my life. My reply was, "you may call me around 8:00 pm. This time is more convenient for me, and this would allow for more time for me to talk with you." Moreover, I did not expect for him to follow through by calling me. I knew by being a classroom teacher, and having been told that we were the last individuals listed on the Educational Hierarchy, until to have from a school board commissioner was just not likely. I had concluded that my having given him my telephone number was another waste of my time. My plan was to forget about it immediately.

The very next evening approximately 8:05 pm, the telephone rang. I rushed and answered, after saying hello, almost breathless, a smooth sounding voice was on the other end of the line, and he said, "I guess I caught you at a bad time." Without hesitation, he identified himself. Having not shown any surprise or disbelief, I composed my stamina, and switched to a very professional mode.

The conversation last for about an hour. At one point, I forgot that he was a commissioner. He shared with me great ideas about what he would like to see happen in our system, and the type of qualifications needed to make them happen. He also talked to me as if he had known me for a very long time. He was very humane and professional during the entire conversation. The conclusion of the conservation ended with the regular jargon, such as it was my pleasure having spoken with you, and I'll be contacting you again soon. This statement was interpreted as if this were not a one time telephone call, but, will be ongoing. It was because of my years of experience with some of the male Professors at my university, I could not help but think what was the real agenda behind this telephone call. Several days went by before he called again.

It was Friday evening at 10:30 pm when the telephone rang. It was he. I was caught totally off guard again. I did not expect to hear from him especially on a Friday night. This time, he did not identify himself, but after listening for a moment, I knew who he was, because he had a unique type of mannerism, even in his voice, unlike any of my social friends. During this conversation, he asked if the two of us could meet at a neutral place and talk in person very soon. I responded by inferring that if this is to occur, we must keep this conversation geared toward education. I felt very pleased with the stage I thought I had set by saying this. He replied by commenting on various concepts in reference to the needs of our school system. This was very normal as I interpreted his statement, because as a new teacher, filled with ideas, and anxiously awaiting to help make a change for the educational growth of our community, inclusively. We both agreed on the time, and identified a very nice hotel lounge away from the city. This was fine with me, because like himself, I did not want anyone I knew to see me talking to him.

The meeting took place as scheduled. Both of us were playing with the time of arrival. It was liked he had radar. I was hoping either one of us would arrive first, and would already be in place. I did not anticipate actually walking in together, which would have indicated or given one the impression that we had come out on a date. Unfortunately, this plan did not work out. He had much more experience that I with arranging these types of meetings. He had arrived first, sat and waited, saw me before I saw him, and pretended that he was just arriving. He even told me that he had just parked. This was too coincidental, because I deliberately was off schedule. In spite of all of my planning, it seemed that I had been caught up in the middle, and had to walk in with him, appearing to have been on a date.

The hotel lounge was practically empty. A couple of men were sitting at the bar, watching the baseball game on TV. The commissioner decided where were to sit. There was a nice cozy table in the far end of the lounge all by itself. It seemed that a magnetic force pulled him directly to that spot. The waiter came over, and we bother ordered orange juice. I noticed that he did not drink alcohol, neither did I. The very first statement that he made was in reference to a sociological point of view. He began by saying, "tell me who are you, and share with me some of things you would like to do." I replied by talking about education. I knew I was a little off beat, but really did not care at the moment, because of previous experience, always reflecting back to my first encounter with my college Professor. He appeared to have been listening very intensively, however, by evidence of his eye contact, and feedback. My conversation was not going in the direction that he had anticipated, so after a while, he very inconspicuously, changed the tone to create a new and more direct format. It was my turn to listen to him. I knew that I could not have allowed any psychological interference to invade my thought processes while he was speaking. He had the type of voice and mannerism that was captivating, and that would also create a pleasant type of environment for anyone to relax and moreover, forget about his title and position. Although, this was very apparent, I put up a conscious effort to maintain my focus, and deep within, kept in mind that that I was in the company of a School Board Commissioner who made decisions for my job. Therefore, whatever the tone was, it was mandatory that all my responses and behavior would be staged also.

Further into the conversation, again he commended me for being such an excellent teacher, and having accepted to serve as a model teacher for other new teachers. He reflected back on the day he visited my classroom. He also very carefully explained the entire school board positions on education and expectations in reference to performance from both teachers and students. During this time of the meeting, every now and then, I would interject occasionally, by asking straight forward questions, as well as making comments on some of the things that he was saying to avoid becoming bored with the one-sided conversation. I was curious to know each of the commissioner's background and qualifications. My thinking was that, if one is to serve as a commissioner, then one should have qualifications that were geared toward the betterment of the school system.

He began to go through the list of the commissioners names, and related in details how and why each commissioner was selected by the Mayor, and approved by the City Council. He explained to me about each commissioner's unique talents and how they could be applicable to helping our educational system. I was impressed with some of their background, I knew it took a lot of diversified talent to collectively help a system that I thought was in distress. However, it concerned me greatly, why some of the individuals appeared to not have anything in common to help our system.

By now, it was getting late, approximately 12:10 pm, I began to realize that this meeting had gone on just a little too long. Even though, I learned a great deal. Nevertheless, I made the first gesture to depart. I picked up my purse, and began to put on my coat, exemplifying all overt indicators that it was time to go, without having to say it. He also said what a pleasure it was to have sat and talked with me. He continued with his compliments. As we both stood from our seats, he said that he did not know what had happened to the time. He made mention of the fact that when one is enjoying himself, time passes rapidly. He walked me to my car, but just before arriving to my car, he said, "by the way, are you married?" I told him no, never was, and I did not have children. I looked at the expression on his face. He appeared to have been very happy to have heard that answer. Nonetheless, I did not concentrate on his reaction at all, as I began to enter my car to depart for home. His last statement was that, we must do time again very soon, and that he would be contacting me within the next few days.

CHAPTER THREE

INTRODUCTION TO THE GROUP

Approximately one month after having met personally with Mr. Commissioner, I received a letter that was sent to my school. I read it very quickly, but could not believe what I had read. I had to re-read it for a better comprehension of the content. The content of the letter was geared toward an invitation for me, along with ten other professionals to become a part of a team to implement a new concept. The new concept was Individual Guided Education, the acronyms were, "IGE." There was nothing in the letter that identified the other team members. This was all new to me. The letter explained that I had been selected by my peers to serve on this team. The most appealing part of the letter was that a substitute would be provided for three days a week, while the team worked out the particulars, and implemented the concepts and principles of IGE. Since I was relatively new in the system, I did not know many colleagues. The letter was signed by an unfamiliar female, and from a department at headquarters that appeared to have been newly created.

The meeting date came faster then I could do any further research, as to what would be role serving on this team. The first meeting was held at a local university. The players were introduced, each was asked to talk for five minutes, about himself or herself. Most participants found this hard to do. This was an opening exercise, created to set the tone for that which was yet to come. During this activity, I was able to learn a lot about each team member. The most important thing that I learned, was that this team was very carefully chosen. The team was a heterogeneous group. There were no members of the team that had duplicates in his/her presentation. I was impressed with the diversity of experience. After the introductions, a university's spokesperson, who was a female with a doctorate began to explain to the group the purpose of having initiated such a group.

It was very clear, that the challenge was going to be interesting. The challenge that was before us, motivated me. My enthusiasm seemed to had risen, as well as my willingness to become actively involved to help implement the concept of this new endeavor. It was never perceived that all of these players were just there, using this concept, for a gateway to future advancement opportunities in the system.

The team was composed of non-titled individuals who had just everyday positions, such as classroom teachers, assistant to an assistant, and some of them appeared to just had positions of errand folks. The teams' academic background included most Bachelors' Degrees, with the exception of two Masters, one of which I held. However, this did not phase me. As mentioned, I was still considered new to the system and young. Everyone on the team was older than I, and had a lot more experience, obviously.

When it was time for discussion, and opportunity for input from the group, I had very little to say. All I knew from what had happened during the orientation process, that this program would be significance for the students. At this meeting, I was not aware that there were two undercover recruiters on this team. If I had known at the time, I would have been a lot more vocal. As the time passed, and meetings continued, the experience players at some point, appeared to have been over performing. Because of my naiveness, I thought that all of their behaviors were sincere, and that they had genuine interest in helping the children in our system.

The meeting was adjourned. Each member hung around, still showing exceptional enthusiasm. I did notice that the two recruiters appeared to have been the center of attraction. However, I did not spend hardly any time with them, because I truly thought that they were a realistic part of the team. I must mention, the two recruiters were both males. Also the gender of the team was composed of two males, and ten females, excluding the two male recruiters.

Before we departed the premises, we knew that the next meeting would be the following week on the same day at the same time, but at a different university. This was fine with me. Although, I was a new teacher, I was already beginning to become bored having to do the same thing every day back at my assigned school. I had been assigned five classes of eight graders. Most of whom had serious disciplinary problems, and were from a single parent home. The only way I kept their attention was by doing a lot of demonstrations, because I was teaching Physical Science. My students appeared not to have been exposed to hardly anything culturally, or outside scientific institutions or museums. Often times, I would let the students get involved. Each Friday, I allowed them to do an experiment of their choice. It was called, "Do Your Thing." The concept derived from the popular song during that time from the Artist, Isaac Hayes. Therefore, after having done this activity for several weeks, to be away for a couple of days per week, created that most needed break for me. This is why I anxiously looked forward to meeting with the newly appointed team for the implementation of IGE.

Prior to the next week's meeting, a lady was scheduled to meet with me. She became my permanent substitute teacher. Her mannerism was very unusual I thought. After talking with her, she told me that she was in training to become a State Trooper. I felt more relaxed after she told me that. I knew how Junior High school Students behaved with substitutes.

The school that I had been assigned had a very negative reputation that had been ongoing for years, the constant fighting every day, and the police cars and wagons to take the students away continuously. On some occasions, security guards had to actually fire weapons in the air to just break up fights, to get the students attention upon the dismissal of school. So, I knew my substitute had to have a lot of strength, firmness, and would have to be aware of this age group behavior at all times. After our meeting, I felt uncomfortable that the substitute and the qualifications that were needed to work with my students. Therefore, I could be a part of this newly appointed team without having to worry about my students back at the school.

The day of the week for the meeting had arrived. I arrived at the university about forty minutes ahead of time. I had to allow time to locate the place. My plan was, if I were too early, I would have had time to just wait in my car, and try to figure out the role that I was going to play that day. Not knowing too much, I could not come up with any strategies, but I knew I had to do more participating in the group. As I sat and observed the environment, I glanced at the other automobiles that were on the parking lot, and to my surprise, one of the team members, a male, was also sitting in his car, and appeared to have been writing notes. He recognized me immediately and spoke. He began to make comments about his reason for having arrived very early. His reason was the same as mine. He said that his residence was very far from the university, and that he did not know how long it would have taken him to arrive. Therefore, this was his reason for arriving early. He appeared to have been at least 15-20 years my senior. We began to discuss some of the concepts and principles that had been presented during the orientation meeting. He seemed to have been more or less interviewing me. It was because of my honesty, I did not hesitate to make comments on any of his questions that were asked. It did not occur to me that he was trying to get more in depth feel about who I was. He must have known that I definitely did not know the undercover purpose of this team, and he was right. Our conversation continued, as other team members arrived. Finally, all team members had arrived, and we all entered as a group in the meeting room.

The meeting began as scheduled. Directing the meeting was a different female. I had never seen her before. During the first few minutes, she made it clear that she was a member of the staff at the university, and extended to the group a most sincere welcome to the university. Ms. B, (to whom I will call her) stressed the importance of having such a team. She demonstrated a very strong desire to become an active member of the group. She appeared to have been overwhelmed with the potential that this group had, as well as the philosophy of implementing such essentials that would include everyone affiliated with education.

During the discussions, I became very actively involved. I could perceive great things happening as the results of this group. One of the most needed thing to have happened was focusing on the student's individual needs. Thus, adhering to the principles of the purpose of the team, IGE, Individual Guided Education.

I had tried to help my students individually already. This has been very difficult to do, because of the very large class sizes. My students were from various types of backgrounds, and lacking in many of the very basic skills. Often time, I would wonder how some of them had even made it to the eight grade, and what criteria had been used to get them there. Anyway, we begun to brainstorm, coupled with trying to maintain realism vs idealism on ways to help the children in the system. Everyone played an active role in this process. The group seemed to have been very serious with their input and suggestions. Some of the suggestions were team teaching, which is teachers working and planning together, and integrating the different disciplines. An example, a English Teacher would help a Science Teacher with how to teach reading skills, a Social Studies Teachers would help a Math Teacher by sharing with him or her how Math could be directly applied to real life situations, instead of just working problems from a textbook, or on a chalk board, the Math Teacher would become more scientifically oriented, and during his or her lessons, would began to think and share with the students why and how such math could be applicable in the science class. I could very well understand these methods. Too often, students could not see the relationship between the disciplines. This certainly would have begun to help students, wholistically with this type of integration.

After the meeting was adjourned, we continued to discuss even more principles and strategies among ourselves that the team could have implemented. The discussions were kept informal. After I left everyone, I began to consider immediately how I could use some of the concepts discussed with my students. The next class meeting, I tried some of these concepts, and they worked very well. I continued with this trend until I became comfortable. I began to discuss with my colleagues who were teaching the same students. My focus was on the MESS Subjects, Math, English, Science and Social Studies. They too, were eagle to try this new concept. We were very motivated to plan lessons to ensure the integration of each discipline. We set up an evaluation and assessment instrument to monitor the significance of our effort. The outcome was outstanding.

As time passed, meetings continued with the group as planned for a while. Slowly, the meeting dates began to cancel. This interrupted the continuity in planning. Finally, I did not receive any more communications about any meetings. I did not have any member of the group telephone number. However, later, I saw a group member at a mall, and she thought I knew why the group had been resolved, but I had no answer for her.

A year had passed. I continued to go the School Board Meetings. I would see on the agenda confirmation and or promotions. From time to time, one of the team members name would appear, until finally, all the team members had been promoted, except for two of us who were both females. I began to become curious as to how this happened, and what criteria had been used. I did not know how to reach the other female. I did know, however, that I would be seeing the Commissioner. Finally, I got enough nerves to call him and inquire about each teach member's promotion. By this time, Mr. B had become very comfortable with talking to me on a personal basis. He said, very frankly, "until you learn how to drop your draws, the chances of your receiving a promotion in this system would not be forthcoming." This statement bewildered me. Little did I know, the real purpose of this team was geared toward SexCessFully Promotions, and not what had appeared to have been focusing on students needs.

After getting over the shock from my response, Mr. Z appeared to have gotten a little angry. I recognized this behavior by his body language that indicated that he was just not use to, or if ever, had anyone to respond to him in such manner. It was obvious that Mr. Z was used to calling the shots, because he was too comfortable and sure of himself. Mr. Z told me that I could never respond to anyone on his level, and with the clot he had again in such manner. In other words, the inference drawn from this statement was that according to my interpretation, teachers should remain silent, and go along with orders from the higher epsilon, regardless of their morals and values, as well as any standards that they may have. This was apparent that teachers were not viewed as individuals by some top officials. In addition, principals also were not given any respect. This was evidence of Mr. Z's plans for the newly formed private social click.

Approximately two hours had passed since the other members departed. Mr. Z appeared to have been in no hurry to go home. I must mention, Mr. Z was married, with several teenage children in the home. Since Mr. Z did not make any move to leave, I began to question him about his staying out so late. I was aware of wives understanding decent hours for their spouses to stay out to attend meetings related to their employment, etc., but I had problems trying to understand how could anyone explain staying out past 1:00 a.m. While sharing this with Mr. Z, he boldly stated that his wife did not ask him any questions. He continued to state that he cooked, ironed and washed for himself. Quiet frankly, Mr. Z indicated that there was not a bonded relationship between the two of them. After having stated that, Mr. Z began to share with me that various educators who had been promoted satisfied his needs, not only sexual, but provided him with his clothes, and paid for other incidentals, such as his doctor's visits, etc.

By now Mr. Z was comfortable with me, until he did not hesitate to call individuals names who were supporting him, and why they were doing so. As he told me these things, he would laugh very frequently. I could feel more pain, stress, and disgust for those individuals who were totally being manipulated by Mr. A just to get a promotion or maintain a position. However, the connection between the educators avoiding Mr. Z would have probably created a negative environment that would have caused them their position or title. Therefore, in my opinion, these individuals were held as hostages. I was still having difficulty in perceiving individuals doing this type of thing just to remain in a position. Mr. Z made it clear that once promoted, or given a title, one had to perform anyway dictated, like it or not. I continued to wonder why some of these individuals continued to be maneuvered. It would have been much better if the individuals would have signed a life-long unlimited behavior type of contract with Mr. Z. Needless to say, Mr. Z never seemed to have been worried, nor shown any concern about these individuals. I could hardly help but think that Mr. Z should have demonstrated some fear of having these people report him, or talking to other people in education, and or elected officials, sharing with them about Mr. Z's behavior. Nonetheless, Mr. Z in search of his own humanity took chances that marked his life career, and did not seem too much concerned about facing subjected inhumane consequences from a society that should have implemented justice.

During the entire time while Mr. Z and I were alone in my house, he never made a direct pass that implied sexual orientation at me. Instead, he was more focused on his organizational strategy for the group members. This somehow surprised me, however. One could have easily assumed that it would have been just the opposite. Mr. Z showed evidence of having organized groups like this before, because he did not stumble or display any overt mistakes.

Finally, Mr. Z asked for his coat, and said that he was going to leave. The time was about 2:30 a.m. I did not realize that it was that late. Mr. Z had the innate ability for keeping one's attention, and or diverting one's attention. I assisted him with his coat. He was very polite and smooth. He opened the door, and turned around, and embraced me. Again, not displaying any sexual orientation. That gesture was in appreciation for my hospitality for the evening. Mr. Z said to me that I was a swell person, and that with further coaching, I would become an excellent student. As he left, he made reference that he would be contacting me very soon. I remained up for another hour after his departure. There had been so many things that had gone down during the evening, until I knew that it would have been difficult for me to retire for bed immediately. I began to analyze, as well as try to digest and make some sense of everything that had happened. I was feeling so overwhelmed, until it was difficult finding the beginning point to begin the analytical process. However, this took several minutes, I finally began with the arrival of each member. Two females had come together. As I thought back, each member appeared to have been in neutral upon his/her arrival. Everyone appeared to have been reserved, not knowing whether to trust each other or me. It was evident that Mr. Z's role was to set the tone, and assume the host role for the evening. I continued to think, still processing very carefully the activities of that evening. I found it very difficult that some of the members would actually follow Mr. Z's directives, as well as go along with his sexual plan just to remain in their current positions, and or get a promotion. My imagination took me through the process of trying to imagine sexual activities between women and women, and men and men. After all, I had never been exposed to this type of activity before. Just to mention, although I knew that any possibility existed as such, but my main problem at the moment was that the stage was being set for the newly formed click to perform these sexual activities. With these thoughts, I realized that I had a serious headache that came as the result of having tried to perceive all of this. I concluded that if Mr. Z's plan had come to fruition, that somehow or some way he should have been reported or exposed. The entire plan was very immoral, insane, and needless to mention disgusting.

CHAPTER FOUR

SEXCESSFULLY PROMOTIONS

(The Introduction)

A few years had passed very rapidly. I was no longer a new teacher. By now, I thought that I had become very knowledgeable about how the system functioned. It was because of previous experience, etc. I thought I had a good grip on everything, thus, knew how the system worked. I thought that by my having witnessed various activities that nothing else could have been done, or even would have been surprising to me. How far from the truth was I thinking.

Moreover, I continued to maintain perfect attendance at the School Board Meetings. I continued to meet new people, and became even more familiar with the regulars. It was to the point, whereas I was beginning to become inducted into the "select" few click. I was receiving invitations to outside of school related activities. i.e. parties, and other social events. Individuals in attendance and part of the click were beginning to feel very comfortable with me and each other. Often times, they would disregard the fact that I was a classroom teacher when they would forever talk negatively about teachers.

One of the original general click, so to speak, derived another click. The click was hand-picked by individuals at the top, and who had one's job at state. This newly formed click was composed of three principals, one teacher (myself), other miscellaneous positions that did not involve school

25

based personnel, but mainly who either had an office at the headquarters, and or with the City and State Government. This click was very well organized. The original click members were not a part of this click. This click was more or less a private social club. It was understood by everyone that anything discussed, and or any type of behavior exemplified would not have been broadcast. Yet, it was O.K. to talk among one another.

Time passed, and the click became even more organized, etc. It became so tight, until once a month we began to meet all together for planning. I lived alone, was single, and no children. I was buying a two apartment house. One of the apartments was empty during that time. My neighborhood was very isolated and secluded, no churches, schools, stores, and only elder homeowners who appeared to have stayed inside the majority of the time. It was decided that this was the perfect place to have the monthly meetings.

At each meeting, each person in the click had been assigned to bring something to my house, whether it was food or a variety of drinks. During the first meeting, I recall very distinctly my having been just a listener and observer. One of the top officials was the director, or if you will "the head person in charged." All who were in attendance were very cool at this meeting. One could detect very easily the reservation from each member of the click. This was the initiation meeting. Everyone seemed to have been feeling the next person out, until the degree level of comfort availed.

Each group member had been given a specific time to arrive at my house. This arrangement was made such that my neighbors would not become suspicious. The top official, I will refer to as Mr. Z arrived last to the first meeting. Upon his arrival, everyone seemed to have been very curious about what would be in store for the evening. Mr. Z's mannerism was such that everyone seemed to have been very comfortable and relaxed. After several minutes, Mr. Z asked if I would show the group the adjacent apartment. As aforementioned, this apartment was free of tenants. Without any reluctance, I showed the apartment to the group. There were no expressions, or indication from any of the members that this was going to be used for SexcessFully Promotions.

Strangely enough, after having toured the apartment, no one made any comments, not even Mr. Z. There was no furniture in the apartment, except for two single chairs. However, there was very nice clean carpet throughout the apart. Also, there was a very large kitchen with all modern appliances, microwave oven, and the bathroom was very spacious, with towels and shower curtains. Nonetheless, after having returned to my living quarters, the group continued with the social hour. After several hours passed, the group decided it was time to depart. I noticed that Mr. Z was acting like more of a host to them then I. He walked them to the door, and thanked them for coming, while implying that he would be contacting them for feedback from the meeting.

All of the members had finally left. Mr. Z and I were the only two left. Mr. Z began to analyze what had happened. He focused on what the possibilities could be between them. Some of the possibilities included a minute reference to education, while the main focus was on sexual activities between members within the group. During this dialogue, Mr. Z very graphically told me that he would be pairing women with women, women with men, and then men with men. He made it very clear that for these group members to either advance in their career, or to remain in their present positions, they would and must follow his directions.

After Mr. Z made this statement, very quickly I came to the realization that I had not seen it all, and that I was still in the embryonic state in reference to how many individuals became promoted, and or were in top positions without having met the qualifications. While Mr. Z was talking, I was deeply concentrating and trying to imagine if some of the group members would have actually adhered to his directions. Most of the group members had wives or husbands. Only two were single, including myself. I asked Mr. Z if he were sure that Ms. A and Ms. C would do a thing like that. These were individuals who carried themselves very well, and whom I admired as great educators. He said, that they would be the main players. Mr. Z continued to refer me as a youngster who had a lot to learn. Although, I did not feel like I was such a youngster. After all, I had graduated from college, working on my Master's, and had been teaching for about five years.

All the time that Mr. Z was talking about what his expectation was from the other members of the group, it appeared that I had been omitted. As the evening passed, I kept using the word, "they." I was not aware that Mr. Z had already made up his mind about my role in this matter. On the other hand, because of my morals and values, I had already concluded that I was not going to participate in this type of behavior, even if it meant resigning from the school system. This is the reason why I kept referring to them as "they" which I continued to use with a conscious effort. After having repeated this word so often, Mr. Z realized that I was letting him know that he was not to include me with his plan. With this in mind, Mr. Z said to me again, with any reservation, "if you don't learn how to drop your draws, you will never be promoted in this system, and that life is going to be very hard for you." Well now, I thought that this statement triggered a bad nerve reaction by me. At this point, very quickly I forgot as well as disregarded Mr. Z's position. I told Mr. Z that I was not going to drop my draws, nor will I tolerate him trying to manipulate and program me just to get a promotion. Although, I must admit, I did not say this in the most pleasant way. I used a few choice words that were really not a daily part of my vocabulary. However, it was imperative that I behaved in such manner, because Mr. Z had already exemplified the he was heartless.

CHAPTER FIVE

(THE PARTY BEGINS)

Time was approaching for the next meeting date. Mr. Z called me one afternoon to confirm the meeting date and time that had been scheduled for the month at my house. I was a bit nervous, even while he asked for the confirmation. I knew that the other members of the group did not have a "clue" in my opinion, what had been planned by Mr. Z for them. It was no way that could reach any of the members to alert them as to Mr. Z's plan before the meeting. I knew where the individuals of the group were located, but could not have taken the chance on contacting them at their schools, or at the headquarters. The reason for not having taken any chances on calling them was that, because this group was very well organized, and that everything discussed among the members had to be kept very confidentially. To protect the interest of all involved, no matter what the appearance may have been in reference to schools telephone lines being private, it was always that one possibility of someone picking up an extension, and or entering into one's office unannounced. This type of action had to be avoided for the protection of all significant others.

CHAPTER SIX

(THE SEXUAL ACTIVITY BEGINS WITHIN THE GROUP)

Approximately one week had passed when my telephone rang, and the caller was none other than Mr. Z. Mr. Z did not hold a lengthy conversation during this call. He got right to the reason for calling. He said that he was calling to make an arrangement for a meeting to take place at my house. Instead of inviting all of the group members this time, he informed me that there will only be three of the members, who would be attending this meeting. It was no doubt in my mind what the real purpose of this meeting must have been. Mr. Z did not bother to identify who the members that would be in attendance. A bit curious by now, I agreed to host the meeting requested by Mr. Z.

Meanwhile, I tried to put together who the participants would have been, and the activity they would have engaged. I could hardly do my job, because this thought process seemed to have dominated my thinking 24/7. Moreover, the meeting was scheduled for one week after Mr. Z had called. Therefore, this thought pattern continued to cause severe stress for me, even to the point where I did not feel like facing the students I had been assigned. This week appeared to have taken a year. This was because of the curiosity and stress that had plagued me.

One could never predict what Mr. Z would do next. As mentioned prior, Mr. Z was heartless, and did not seem to have been operating using a conscious. Morals and values were not a part of his make-up. I must admit that although I do not condone this type of behavior, Mr. Z never exemplified any stress. He always appeared to have been very happy and "jolly-go-lucky."

Three days had passed, and there was no telephone call from Mr. Z. I thought that he would have called just to see if anything had come up in my schedule that would have canceled, or interfered with this meeting. Unfortunately, Mr. Z demonstrated the role of a dictator. He was so confident at doing such, until most individuals who were in his presence appeared to have been intimidated with his mannerism. These individuals had to live with continuous fear, because Mr. Z, after all, was a School Board Commissioner, as well as in the Mayor's pocket who appointed him. Since all of the group members were in education, we knew we had to remain very cool, and that we could never rub Mr. Z the wrong way. Also, we knew by now, how treacherous Mr. Z was or could have been. He would from time to time overtly let one know the indicators that were involved. The indicators, unfortunately were not about the real focus, the children, but were directly related to any individual who would have violated his command. He would let one know that his or her job would have been in serious jeopardy if such would have occurred.

Friday finally came. While at school during the day, I was just a nervous wreck, needless to mention, the lacking of rest the night before. All I could think about was what Mr. Z had planned for the evening. I knew that if he made plans for me to become sexually involved, somehow, I was not going to do it. Mr. Z had already told me that he was only inviting just three of the group members. This was a very odd number, I thought. I had always presumed that if sexual activities were to take place during this time, then what would be the nature of them. Because of my naiveness again, I was thinking in reference to sexual activities that would be a twosome, etc. For this reason, that was why I could not sleep and function normal prior to this meeting, because of having to worry about if Mr. Z had made plans for me to make the even number four to create two couples.

The trend of thought pattern continued to dominate my mind, that also triggered malfeelings within me. Because of these malfeelings, I noticed that I was somewhat dysfunctional. I did not feel like going to my school and teaching anything. The students appeared to have been more annoying than usual. Moreover, during the afternoons and evenings, while at home. I did not have the energy to talk on the telephone to my social friends. I tried to avoid this activity, because of the fear that I would have let on to others what was about to happen.

Time was approaching very quickly for the arrival of my guests for the evening. I was pacing from one room to another, checking and rechecking to make sure that everything was in order. Under normal circumstances, usually I did not vacuum the carpet in the empty apartment. However, that afternoon, I rushed home and vacuumed the empty apartment that was about to be used by my guests.

The sun had set. The time was approximately 7:30 p.m. I recall hearing a faint doorbell sound. Not too sure that I had heard the bell, I went to the door to just check. There stood facing my storm door were two very well dressed females. One of which was a principal, (Ms. A who I will refer) and the other (Ms. B) who was an assistant to Mr. Y, who was located at headquarters. Both of these females were very pleasant, very charming, and exemplified a lot of sophistication and class. They embraced me as they entered into my living room. I offered them something to drink. Both of them seemed to have been very relaxed, without any worry or anticipation of what was yet to come. I was still very nervous. The conversation was very generic. No one mentioned Mr. Z. There was not even a comment in reference to when he was expected to arrive.

At this time, I was still trying to analyze and digest, using serious speculation that which had been planned by Mr. Z for these females for the evening. I was wondering if Mr. Z had previously informed each of them what to expect, and or what role they would be performing for the evening. I tried to observe their mannerism in such fashion to depict any kind of obvious hint, but the two females remained very cool, and nothing ever became apparent from their action that they knew what was to be expected from them during this visit.

As we sat and conversed, we paused briefly, because we all seemed to have heard someone walking outside, appearing to have been approaching my porch. My heart must have skipped several beats at that time. The doorbell rang, I did not hesitate to respond, because of my nervousness. At the door, was none other than Mr. Z. He was filled with smiles as I invited him inside. I was so nervous, until I hurriedly rushed him inside where the females were seated in my living room. I noticed the he did not bother to embrace anyone as he sat alone. I offered him something to drink, he refused the offer.

Mr. Z did not hesitate to get right to the point as to the purpose of the meeting. He began telling us of the sexual fantasies that individuals had, but were too afraid to live them out. He looked at both Ms. A and B, and told them that the two of them were examples of what he meant about folks who had sexual fantasies, but had always been afraid to experiment with them. He continued his conversation by telling them that each of them always wanted to experience having sex with another female. Both Ms. A and B were married with children. To my surprise, Ms. A and Ms. B just kept silent, while Mr. Z continued with the dialogue. I still could not believe what I was hearing. Mr. Z told the two females that the purpose of their being at my house that night was to provide the opportunity for both of them to live out their sexual fantasy. He began to tell them exactly what each role would be. He told them they were to perform oral sex on each other. Still, there was no reaction from the two females. He made it very clear that no one would ever know about what happened, but the four of us who were in attendance.

Mr. Z finished setting the stage for the females. He said to them, "let's go upstairs," which was to the empty apartment. We all went upstairs to the empty apartment, and went into the living room area. He directed each of us to sit. There was no furniture in this room, so the females had to sit on the floor. He asked if I would provide a couple of bath clothes and soap. The bathroom was empty, I came to my living area to get towels. When

I returned with the items, I placed them in the living room. I hesitated for a moment before I went where the guests were, fearing what I would see. With enough courage, finally I returned to the living room. It was obvious during my brief absence the females had been directed by Mr. Z to remove their clothing. They had taken off all of their clothes, except for their panties and bra. Mr. Z was still fully dressed.

Mr. Z looked at the two, and reminded them that the time was getting a little late, and said that they had better get on with the party. Both Ms. A and B took the remaining of their clothing items off, and laid down on the floor, began to embrace each other passionately. It was no time before Ms. A began to perform oral sex on Ms. B. Mr. Z removed all of his clothing, while coaching them along by repeating all kind of sexual obscenities. The two females kept very quiet, all I could hear was just the sound from their bodies contact. After Mr. Z allowed this activity to go on for about 15 minutes, he told Ms. A that was enough. He looked at Ms. B and told her that it was her turn. Mr. Z appeared to have built and imaginary clock. Ms. B reversed the role as ordered by Mr. Z without hesitation. Mr. Z's behavior continued as before. Mr. Z told Ms. B that her time was up after about 15 minutes. No one was talking by now.

When I actually saw Ms. A began to have oral sex with Ms. B, I went to the bathroom and vomited. In all of my years of living, I had never seen anything so demeaning in all of my life. It was not just the oral sexual performances that caused my nausea, but more or less how these females had allowed Mr. Z to have dictated to them what they had to do, perhaps, against their morals, religion, and values just to maintain a position, and or to receive a promotion.

While the females were still nude, as well as Mr. Z, they were told by Mr. Z that each would have to perform oral sex on him, he was still standing. I noticed that he refused to lie on the floor. He told them to just get on their knees and perform. Each female performed oral sex on him about 10 minutes each. During the time of this activity, no one said anything. I really wanted to express my sincere feeling to all of them in reference to their behavior, but I was too afraid as to the consequences that would have been in store for my future in education. I had to be extremely careful, because I knew that Mr. Z was telling the truth when he made it clear that he could make my life very pleasant, and or very unpleasant during my tenure in education. I could not take any chances on calling his bluff, because I was already convinced that Mr. Z was heartless. In addition, to make matters worse, I could not tell anyone about what had happened, not even my very close friends, because they were also teachers. If I had told anyone, my greatest fear was that in no way they would have believed me. I knew that I would have been categorized and labeled as a sincere "trouble-maker" or even a "lunatic." Although, deep within my heart, I believed that they would have suspected that I would have been telling the truth.

Nonetheless, Ms. A and B prepared to clean themselves to regroup to depart, and return to their normal life style. Meanwhile, Mr. Z made no attempt to do anything. He did put his clothes back on. After the two females had dressed, there was little or no dialogue between anyone. I was baffled. I did not know where to begin a conversation after having witnessed this type of behavior. I was thinking the entire time, however about how the two females must have felt. They knew I had seen their activities, as well as knew the role that both had in the school system. They appeared to have not been embarrassed or had any fear in reference to what could have easily been on my mind, and if I would ever tell anyone what had happened.

The two females knew it was time to go home. The time was approximately 11:00 p.m. They politely stated that they were leaving. Each thanked me for my hospitality. They looked at Mr. Z, and told him that they looked forward to hearing from him very soon. This statement aroused my curiosity. I did not know if this statement meant that Mr. Z had promised them some type of reward for the activity that they had done, or if they actually had enjoyed the oral sex between the two of them, and were expecting for Mr. Z to make future arrangements for this type of activity to be ongoing. Mr. Z responded to them in a nonchalant manner that could have mentally made confirmation to their statement, or perhaps, "he had finished with them" type statement.

Mr. Z remained after the two females had departed. By now, I was still in a state of shock and disbelief of what I had seen. Therefore, I had to make reference to the activity to Mr. Z. I began by telling him that I would not believe that those two women were bold enough to do such a thing, especially in front of me, a teacher. Mr. Z responded by firstly, calling them the "B" word, whom he referred to both of them. He said those "B's" always wanted to do that, because their husbands were no longer satisfying them sexually, and that had made them very arrogant. Therefore, he stated that was why he had made the arrangement for them to try something new and loosen up, hoping that this would help to have deleted some of their frustration and arrogance. It was clear from this statement what Mr. Z thought about women. He showed absolutely no remorse or respect for them, and appeared to have thought all females were "B's." While continuing to talk to Mr. Z, his behavior exemplified what had just happened to be very funny. He kept a smile on his face the entire time that he talked. He was very obviously glowing over his control and power that he clearly used, manipulating others, using major undertone threats to their jobs if they did not follow his dictation.

CHAPTER SEVEN

THE RENAISSANCE

(For Better or Worst)

Three years had passed, and there seemed to have been further deterioration in the school system. The standard test scores continued to have gotten lower, and the drop-out-rate had increased. These results stimulated the Elected Officials to work on making a change within the school system so that they could get re-elected. From my observations, most of the elected officials based their campaign platform on how they had planned to improve the school system, once they were elected.

The school system during this time was in such turmoil, it would have been very difficult for the Elected Officials who were currently in office to have been re-elected without making promises to make changes in the educational system. It was very clear that no one seemed to have made a difference, needless to mention, contributed to the rehabilitation of education. It was because for these reasons, the decision was made for a renaissance to take place. This renaissance was to begin at the top to try to change the image of the school system.

The search was on for a new executive, and new commissioners. Individuals from all over the nation were sending in their credentials. I read the criteria for the executive's position, and one of the components of these criteria was that the person who would be appointed much have an earned doctorate. I continued reading more about the qualifications, and the way they were written, were very discouraging for the more tenured educators in the school system. One discouragement was that the warning an applicant not to apply for the position, if he or she did not have an earned doctorate. All, and or any other qualifications would have not been given any consideration for the position.

Mr. Z still was on board. He had been assigned by an Elected Official to serve on the newly formed Search Committee for the Executive's Position. Meanwhile, Mr. Z had continued to contact me. Mr. Z was also a part of another influential committee that was very instrumental in making decisions in reference to the operation of the city. This group was very powerful, and affected many departments in the city, not just education.

The evening news continued to broadcast about the need for this renaissance to occur within the school system, while keeping everyone up-to-date as to whatever progress had been made with the committee search. By this time, I had met many scholars in education. Some had made many outstanding contributions to education throughout their tenure. Some of them would contact me from time to time, and I would encourage them to apply for the position. Many of them had received a doctorate. Unfortunately, if the one female, in my opinion, had been elected to this position, I am convinced that she could have made a phenomenal change for the betterment in our system, but she did not have a doctorate, although she was already in a top position. I did not matter to the Search Committee that she had earned post graduate credits, and that she was currently in an administrative position.

I knew her background, and was very familiar with her skills, qualifications, and the contributions that she had made for many years in education, very emphatically, I encouraged her to apply for the executive position. She was very reluctant to complete all of the paper work needed for the position. After having continued to pressure her (Ms. D, I will call her), she finally applied for the position.

The deadline for the applicants was nearing. Everyone involved seemed to have been very enthusiastic about the change in the system that was yet to come. To adhere to the standard formality, the applicants who had submitted all required documents were interviewed after the process of elimination of those who did not meet the criteria advertised. Moreover, during this time, I was really not too concerned about having to witness anymore distasteful, and immoral activities in reference for promotions. However, after having gotten very comfortable with this type of thinking, and for the first time, I was beginning to feel somewhat more relaxed, my telephone rang. It was none other than Mr. Z. Mr. Z told me that he had scheduled a meeting at my house that would include one of the candidates who had applied for the Executive's Position, as well as other influential individuals who would have formed an undercover interviewing panel. He informed me that the agenda for the even would consist of a mean, and alcoholic beverages. Mr. Z was laughing while he was telling me about the agenda. He continued telling me even more details about the agenda, and said that he would be preparing the food.

In my living quarters, there was a kitchen on a lower level, isolated from the living room. Mr. Z told me that he would be preparing the food, and my role would be to entertain the selected interviewing panelist to make sure that they would be drinking plenty of the alcoholic beverages. His rationale was to make the very drunk so that it would have been easier for him to manipulate them.

I did not know that Mr. Z and others had already decided on who they really wanted to fill the position for the school system executive position at this point of the game. Although, I knew from previous observations, that whomever this candidate was, he/she would have to pay a price, because I was convinced by now, that Mr. Z's personnel always became the victim of his manipulation. I knew it was a price they paid. As I thought that I could relax, the arrangement made by Mr. Z once again, to invite guests to my house, re-instated the fear, stress and even more mal feelings about our school system, and the way decisions were being made.

Back at my assigned school, I always felt that I was on stage, and had to be very careful to whom I would allow to be in my company. This was a very difficult task for me. I did not know if Mr. Z had someone at my school who had been assigned to watch me, and report back to him. This fear became so overwhelming within me, until I became a recluse, coupled with just pretending that I was always busy in my classroom. I avoided going into the teachers' lounge and cafeteria. At the faculty meetings, I would intentionally arrive late, so that I could sit on the side to avoid having any conversation with my colleagues.

A few days before the meeting had been schedule to take place at my house, (the interview) I contacted Ms. D, trying very carefully not to have let on that this meeting had been scheduled. It was my hope that Ms. D had been selected the female to have been interviewed. I recall asking Ms. D if she had received any feedback from the search committee, and if so, what was the possibility of her being selected for the position advertised. Ms. D informed me that she was still waiting, and that she had not heard from anyone, or had received confirmation of the receipt of her documents.

The information that Ms. D provided during our conversation confirmed that she had not been the person invited to my house for the undercover interview with the decision-making elites. However, during our dialogue, I was very careful not to drop a hint to her that a meeting had been scheduled. Whereas, I was somewhat sure that during this meeting, the final decision for the position would have been made. My conclusions of such thinking was based on the individuals who were invited to make-up the interviewing panel. Each of them held very powerful positions. It was most unlikely that whatever their decision would have been, there would not have been any questions asked.

Mr. Z kept all of us in fear continuously. The fear, stress and angry were really beginning to interfere with my performance at my school. Regardless, to the kind of activity that I was involved, the thoughts of all of the behaviors I had observed always were the dominating factor that kept me mentally preoccupied. I recall attending faculty meetings, looking at my colleagues and hoping that they would never find out the corruption that was going on in the school system. Also, as I would look at each staff member, I would imagine what type of possibility each had, and or what each would have to do to advance or get promoted in the system.

In addition, if this advancement were to occur, would it be the results of a SexCessFully Promotion.

The day of the week for the meeting had finally arrived. Mr. Z had called earlier and said, the he would be arriving first to discuss some particulars with me before the other guests arrived. It was about 4:30 p.m. on Friday when Mr. Z arrived at my house. Mr. Z was carrying two bags of groceries, and had to return to his car to get the remaining of the items that he had purchased. I noticed that he had a large bag from a liquor store. I helped him with the items. I was curious as to what type of alcohol he had purchased. Mr. Z had told me earlier that he did not drink. Mr. z had purchased very strong alcoholic beverages. Also included in the purchase were other items to make mixed drinks. I did not know anything about making or mixing drinks, because I did not drink. He told me that my job would be to make the drinks. I laughed, and told him that I did not have a "clue" what went with what. He laughed also, and said that he didn't either. He continued laughing and said that between the two of us, we will fix them up just fine.

Mr. Z began to make preparations to cook the food. He re-emphasized that he did not want me around him while he was preparing the food. He told me that my job was to stay upstairs with the guests, keep them supplied with drinks. By the way, the applicant who had been scheduled two hours after the "elites" had arrived. One could have easily understood the rational for the directive, because after having drank those potent alcoholic beverages, one should have been drunk, or very intoxicated after having drank continuously for two hours.

The guests arrived, and after having welcoming them into my home, immediately I offered them a drink. The guests were coming from their perspective place of employment, and welcomed a drink to unwind. The guests were two females, and one male, all Caucasians ethnicity. Each guest represented a different integer from society. One guest was from the State Department, another from the City Government, and the other was an Elected Official.

I was somewhat nervous when I saw them, but I had to maintain my stamina, and dared to have let on of such behavior. Meanwhile, I continued to follow Mr. Z's direction by deliberately not offering them any food stuff, or any other type of munches while they drank. I am not too sure if at that time, that it was comical or pitiful as I prepared each a drink. Mr. Z did not assist with this, because as mentioned before, he did not know how to prepare drinks, nor did I. So I just used basic common sense, and mixed up a few drinks. However, I did have enough insight, and shred with the guests the type of drinks that we had, and asked what would they prefer and how. This information helped with the preparation tremendously.

The guests appeared to have been very pleased with the outcome of my effort of preparing the drinks. I played the role as if I knew exactly what I was doing, and was a "pro" at doing it. As they drank, I observed physical signs of relaxation and comfort. They became even more friendly, laughing more, thus the entire change in atmosphere.

At last Mr. Z signaled for me to come down into the kitchen. He had finished cooking, and had set the table. I was surprised with the way he had set the table. Everything was out of order. He had taken my most undesirable dishes and placed them on the table. I told him we had to change the set-up. He told me I was not to interfere with anything that he had done. He ordered me to return back upstairs to escort the guests to the kitchen. Upon entering the kitchen, the guests were really laughing and having fun. Immediately they commended Mr. Z how excellent everything looked, as well as making more comments on the smell of the food that he had prepared. During the time all of this was going on, I felt like putting a paper bag over my head to prevent such severe affixation. Each guest sat at the table and began to eat. Mr. Z did not bother to sit, nor did I with the guests. Mr. Z demonstrated first-class hospitality to them in the meantime.

While the guests appeared to have been comfortable eating, the doorbell rang. The applicant finally had arrived. The applicant was a female, (I will call Ms. L). I was very shocked to see who it was, because I knew that she did not have a doctorate that was required for the position advertised. However, Ms. L was exceptionally well dressed, and extremely classy. Ms.

L had all the characteristics shown outwardly that would have looked great at social affairs, and for any type of media presentation.

I didn't hesitate to welcome Ms. L to my home. I made reference that the other guests were present, but they were downstairs eating dinner. I extended the invitation to her to join them, but she declined. I offered her a drink, again, she said that she was just fine and declined. Ms. L obviously had been previously coached by Mr. Z, the type of behavior that he expected from her during this meeting. Although Ms. L was very calm, and appeared to have been very relaxed, she did not show any evidence of having the least worry or anxiety about what had been planned for her role for the evening.

After the guests had finished eating, they returned upstairs to the living room. Ms. L was sitting alone. I was curious to see what was going to happen once they saw Ms. L. Each guest greeted her as if they had known her for a long time. It was no signs of just having met her. Initially, the dialogue between everyone was simply insignificant. This appeared to have been just a minute motivational activity. Without exerting too much energy and effort, there was a smooth transition in reference to the concepts of the conversation. The guests, without hesitation began to start the interview with Ms. L. I did not bother to leave the room, because after all, it was my house. I was very eager to see to what extinct the conversation would go with my presence.

Everyone knew that I was a classroom teacher. None of this knowledge had any effect on the guests. They continued with the interview with Ms. L. I remember the guests asking Ms. L, testing her strength, I believe, if she would have become aware of an incompetent employee in the school system, how would she handle him or her. Ms. L answered very quickly and precisely, appearing to have not given the question any thought. Her reply was that she would see to it that the person would be terminated from the school system. There were no options, nor did she use any other methods that could have been used to avoid the dismissal of the employee. All of the guests seemed to have loved her answer. I looked at Mr. Z, he showed no reaction, either approval or disapproval to Mr. L's response.

The guests did not talk to Ms. L about serious educational issues, nor did they ask if she had been chosen for the position, what plans would she implement to improve the total image of such a distressed school system. The interview last about one-half hour. After which, the conversation was switched briefly back to a more social type of dialogue. Time was getting late for the guests, and all of them prepared to depart. Before their exit, they thanked Mr. Z and me for hosting the meeting, and told Ms. L that she would be hearing from them very soon.

After the guests left, Mr. Z, Ms. L and I were alone. Mr. Z began to explain to Ms. L what some of the inferences that were exemplified from the guests. He told her that they liked her answers, and he, too, was very pleased with the way she had behaved. Mr. Z in essence, confirmed that Ms. L was going to be selected for the position. Ms. L showed no expression, nor a smile, and or gave any feedback to Mr. Z's comments. She appeared to have already known that this was a "done" deal.

After having cleared the air with Ms. L, Mr. Z asked if he could see her downstairs alone. It was no need for me to tag along. At this point, I was too exhausted, and no longer wanted any company in my house. Ms. L did not show any resistance to Mr. Z's request. Without hesitation, they both went downstairs. Downstairs in my house was a family room, bathroom, kitchen and laundry room. In the family room, there was a queen size sleeper sofa. While Mr. Z and Ms. L were in the family room, I could hear various sounds that appeared to have been sounds of kissing or a sexual intercourse. I never bothered to try to see what was happening between the two. There was no talking, until about an hour later. Both of them returned upstairs, and prepared to leave. Mr. Z and Ms. L thanked me for the hospitality and left.

Again, I was left performing the role and an analyst. I was very curious as to if the decision had just been made in my house to select the executive for the school system, as well as if there would have been no further interviews with the other applicants. Also, I recalled the popping sounds that I had heard while Mr. Z and Ms. L were downstairs in my house. I could not help but think conclude that perhaps I had just witnessed another SexCessFully Promotion.

A week had passed since the meeting at my house. Each day, the evening news would update everyone as to what, if any, the progress of the Search Committee. As I would watch the news, I could not help but feel how deceptive the reports were. Although, the reporters were only reporting what they had been told. It was already clear that the decision for the position had been made. Back at my school, my colleagues made comments that showed concerns about what the distressed school system needed. I would feel very badly listening to them, because I knew what the outcome was already, and perhaps who was going to be selected as the next executive for the school system.

Educators continued to wait for the news that would have announced the executive selected. I recall very distinctly, that on a Wednesday, at the top of the evening news, the reporter said that they had heard from the Search Committee, and that they were not ready to choose an executive from the top three candidates. The news reporter stated that the final candidate would be named on the coming Friday. The reporters flashed the names of the final three candidates for the executive position on the television screen, while they gave a brief synopsis of each. The finalists were two males, and one female. The female was Ms. L. I strongly felt that the two male names were just presented as a ploy to divert one's attention from Ms. L. Ms. L did not have a doctorate, as well as was not exactly a household name that one would have easily recognized for her contributions in education to the school system. I might mention that Ms. L was from another stare, and was new to the school system.

I could have easily made a bet that when the candidate's name was announced on the evening news on Friday, it would have been Ms. L. Meanwhile, in the educational environment, discussion of the candidates who everyone had seen on television was ongoing. Almost 100% of the outcome of the discussions was focused on one of the male candidates. I do not recall anyone saying that he/she thought that Ms. L would have been chosen. As a matter of fact, the comments that were made in reference to Ms. L were that individuals could not understand how she had made the final list from the list of other qualified applicants.

Before the announcement was made, I telephoned my friend, the principal, whom I had previously urged to apply for the position. She informed me that she was never called for an interview. However, she stated that she had received a letter from the Search Committee thanking her for her interest in the position, but unfortunately, she did not meet all of the qualifications for such a position, that was having a doctorate degree. The letter, according to her, also commended her on all of her outstanding contributions that she had made in the school system, and wished her continuous success.

Friday had seemed to have arrived very quickly to educators, because this was the day that we knew the announcement was going to be made for the executive's position. While at my school, all were continuing to speculate on which one of the candidates would have been chosen. My colleagues continued to focus on one of the male candidates, never anticipated the possibility of the selection of Ms. L. At the close of school, I rushed around town to take care of some chores so that I would be home in time to watch the evening news. Somehow I had very nervous feelings all week after I had seen the finalists on television. This feeling was the results of the flashback that dominated my mind, because of the meeting with Ms. L and the guests that had taken place previously at my house.

Five minutes just before the evening news came on, I began to pace very nervously in my house. My telephone rang, I did not answer it, fearing that I would have exploded. At the top of the news was the Search Committee has finally selected the candidate for the school system's top executive. After the commercial break, the news reporter said that, "we have received notice from the Search Committee, stating that they were pleased to have selected Ms. L for the school system's executive." I remember saying out loud, "oh my God, I can't believe that I had just witnessed another SexCessFully Promotion.

CHAPTER EIGHT

EXECUTIVE FAILURE

(Disappointments in the System Increased)

By way of conversations, educators seemed to have all been talking about the same subject, which was why did the Search Committee select Ms. L. We knew that the school system needed an exceptional skilled person to help to improve the negative image that our school system was undergoing. It appeared that from the results of listening to everyone's conversations, that this Search Committee had made a mistake by selecting Ms. L. However, some educators knew that they did not have any input into this discussion or could they have made any impact at all if they had written letters, and or used any other type of petitions to inform the Search Committee of their feelings about having selected Ms. L for search distressed school system. Instead, they decided to try to focus on becoming a little more optimistic, and were wishing for the best for the employees and children in the school system that was undergoing major problems.

While eating dinner on the following Tuesday, my telephone rang. On the line was a very low-keyed disappointing sounding voice. It was the principal lady who had been rejected, declined, and dismissed applicant by the Search Committee for the supporting executive's position. Throughout the conversation, she implied that she just could not believe what had just happened. She frequently referred back to the letter that she had received that very clearly informed her of the qualifications that were required for the position, and that an earned doctorate degree was a "must" for the candidate selected for the position. The lady principal voice was evident of disbelief, while expressing sincere concern about the integrity of the Search Committee and the school system.

During our conversation, my heart seemed to have beat very irregularly, because I knew how Ms. L had received that promotion. I was there with selected members from the Search Committee, but, no way, I could say anything to anyone, fearing the consequences that I could have undergone. This was very stressful for me. I could hardly help but feel like a hypocrite. Often times, I would wish for something mystical to happen that would have given me an opening to just tell the truth to everyone about how Ms. L had received that promotion. Unfortunately, this opportunity never availed. The school system was very tight, politically.

It seemed that individuals had been assigned to watch one another, with having knowledge that this was going on. It was very difficult to trust anyone. I recall one of the males who was in an executive position at the headquarters, telling me how lonely he was being at the top. He said that in his position, he could not trust anyone. He would frequently call me at home from his private office just to vent. He told me that he did not know who had been assigned to report on whom, and that once in his type of position, one could not have ever been too careful. He even suspected that his "right-hand" person had been assigned as a reported to other sources that could have been detrimental to his position had he slipped, or behaved in any manner that was not pleasing to the higher epsilon.

Conversations about Ms. L's recent promotion seemed to have been more calmed by now as the time passed. Ms. L made a smooth transition in the supporting executive's position. Hardly anyone knew when she actually began her duties and responsibilities. There were no immediate results or change in the school system under her assistant. Everything was about the same, but each day appeared to have been getting worst.

The following two weeks had seemed to have passed rather quietly, until educators in the system received a memo from headquarters. The memo appeared that the school system was preparing to undergo a metamorphosis.

Most of the information in the memo was geared toward teachers. This was the beginning of using the word, "accountability." The memo outlined criteria for teachers to be held more accountable. Unfortunately, there was nothing in the memo that would have helped teachers with their needs in order to become accountable. There was no mention of the reduction in class size, purchasing the adequate supplies and equipment for each discipline, and never was there any mention of any type of incentives for the teachers who would have effectively met the stated criteria. Teachers, however, did not appear to have gotten excited or showed any enthusiasm after having received this memo. They knew that if all of the criteria were to be met, there should have been additional information included in the memo.

Most teachers were used to individuals at the top blaming them when things were not going well in the system. Teachers knew that they did not have any jurisdiction on student's performance on standardized tests, as long as folks at the top kept re-directing money in different places, except for the classrooms. In addition, included in the memo was information regarding a new evaluation instrument that had to be written for teachers. This was how the individuals at the headquarters had planned to test for teachers accountability. All of these ideas were fine with the teachers. No one seemed to have attested to any of the criteria that were soon yet to happen for them, even though there was no mention of a pay increase for teachers. By remaining silent, it was understood that teachers were compassionate to the higher epsilon demands.

After having discussed such change with some of my colleagues, we all seemed to have been in agreement, that it was time for a change, and that we would not do anything to stop any progress, anything else that would have helped the students. Nonetheless, I kept having flashbacks about the meeting at my house when Ms. L was interviewed. It was very difficult for me to respect any type of memos, and or commands from the top. Often times, I wished that I had never seen the various activities and behavior of individuals from headquarters, because of the stress, angry and fear that these observations had caused. Needless to mention, having to be around my colleagues daily, when I knew what they had no idea of how some things worked in the system.

I would fringed at some of my colleagues after having listened to them, venting their frustration about the school system. To make matters worse for me, I could not tell them the truth. I had to pretend from time to time that I did not know what was going on at the top as well. Each time that I did such, I would experience a very bad feeling on the inside. Even though, all of my life, I had attended church. I was very familiar with the Spiritual teachings and doctrines. As I would reflect back on the doctrines that were geared toward the truth and honesty, I would find myself praying even more, while entertaining the thought as to why my Creator had allowed me to be exposed to all of this pain that early in my career. Although I was aware that everything is done for a reason, and that it was a time and place for everything. Moreover, as a new teacher, this was still very difficult for me to perceive. There was no one assigned to help me with the stress that had come upon me. As a matter of fact, stress was not a popular household word during that era.

A year had passed, and there was no change in the school system, except for what appeared that things were getting worst. However, there had been a committee formed to create a new teacher's evaluation instrument. I was not too sure who made up this committee, or what type of background and educational experience this committee had. The committed worked tirelessly for several months to make sure that they had covered all grounds of justice for teachers.

Finally, the committee had finished it's task. Nevertheless, this was not the end for the teachers' evaluation final call. Part two of this phase was that another group was chosen to evaluate and edit what the previous committee had done. I remember receiving a telephone call at my school from headquarters. It was a strange gentleman's voice. He told me that he had been instructed by Mr. Z to contact me to serve on this hand=picked group of individuals to finalize the teachers' evaluation. The gentleman shared with me the beginning date, place and time that all of this were to take place. In his directions, he made it clear that this entire process had been estimated to last for approximately three days, which was fine with me. This provided a break for me from the classroom. It was difficult for a teacher to last very long at the school to which I had been assigned, without taking frequent breaks. Thus, this opportunity to serve on this committee was sincerely welcomed.

With much enthusiasm and anticipation, I could hardly wait for that Wednesday to arrive, the day that had been scheduled for the meeting. The days for the process for finalizing the teachers' evaluation instrument had been set for the following week, Wednesday thru Friday. Somehow, it appeared that I had more energy, less stress, and did not have time to concentrate on the degree of fear that I was experiencing. Meanwhile, I could hardly help but wonder about who had been set-up-now, and what was the bottom line. During this time in education, I had witnessed so much wrong doing, undercover strategies, and SexCessFully Promotions, until I had problems with trusting anything, anymore in the school system. I had adopted the same attitude of an executive who had told me that it was not wise, needless to mention, very foolish to trust anyone at headquarters. Therefore, my mental status at this point was to question and analyze everything, even asked myself, why I had been selected to serve on this evaluation committee for the teachers. Although I was not a member of the group that bargained for the teachers, this was somewhat strange that anyone would have asked me to so such a task. Particularly, when there were thousands of teaches, who were paying dues to belong to a bargaining agent.

It was Tuesday evening, and while at home, I didn't exactly know what to expect for the Wednesday's activity. To the best of my ability, I tried to relax, to prevent from having to show that I was somewhat skeptical, once I arrived at the headquarters on Wednesday morning. However, I must mention, when I told one of my colleagues on the same staff at the school to which I had been assigned, that I had been selected to serve on this committee, she responded very negatively. I thought that I could trust her. Little did I know that she was going to tell the principal, trying to find out, why I had been selected to serve on this committee. She was a very close friend of the principal. To my surprise, when she inquired about my having been chosen to the principal, the principal's response was that he had learnt very early in his educational career not to question anything that came from headquarters. The female came back and told me what she had done, and how the principal had responded. She told me the principal's exact words were, "I don't give a damn what she (referring to myself) does." When the female told me that, it was clear that the principal had been a victim also of the school system, and he, too, was very angry with how the system functioned.

It was Wednesday morning, my alarmed sound as usual. Upon awakening, my thought patter was dominated with anxiety and curiosity of the meeting that was scheduled for the day. As I dressed, I noticed that I was experiencing some uncomfort in my abdominal area. I had tried to avoid becoming very nervous. I was very much aware that I had become a "time-bomb", ready to explode. After I left my house, I said a prayer, hopefully, that would have helped me through that day, and to keep me calm.

Upon arriving at the headquarters, the morning crowd was beginning to arrive, appearing to be happy and eager to get on with the business of the day. As I observed them, flashbacks of SexCessFully Promotions came over me, as they entered into the building. I didn't know whether to believe if these individuals were actually happy, or very pitiful, and had to fake such disguise. I had not been given specific directions as to where to go for the meeting that had been scheduled. All I knew was that the male name who had called me. I asked the receptionist for his officer number, and followed her directions. I hesitated, took a deep breath before knocking on his door. It was very quiet and peaceful on the floor that his office was located. I knocked very lightly. I could hear a faint movement inside the office. I knew that I was probably at the right place. I waited at the door over a minute before someone opened it. The person who came to the door was a male. (Mr. T, I will call him) We both said good morning, and introduced ourselves. He politely invited me inside, and asked me to sit. In front of the office was an executive desk and a couple of chairs. He said that he was waiting for another person to arrive. Mr. T didn't bother to initiate a conversation, but he did offer coffee. It was great to have the time to sip on the coffee to relax. During the waiting period, I would slyly glance at Mr. T sipping on my coffee, and trying to process some thought process as to where to begin. Mr. T was going through a lot of mail, and other papers that were on his desk. I had seen Mr. T at the school Board Meetings, but had never held a conversation with him. Trying not to initiate a conversation, I made mention having seen him at the meetings. Mr. T in reply to this comment only gave a gesture of confirmation that he did attend all the School Board Meetings as required by his position.

Approximately ten minutes had passed, and the door opened, it apparently was the other person who Mr. T was expecting. This person was a male. (Mr. A I will call him) Mr. A was one of the executives at headquarters. I would always see Mr. A at the School Board Meetings also. Mr. A recognized me immediately from attending the School Board Meetings as well. I saw Mr. T's attitude change abruptly, to be more genuine and friendly. After the arrival of Mr. A, I was turned off somewhat by Mr. T's behavior, because I had been in Mr. T's office for a while, and he had not shown any of the characteristics. The preliminary dialogue between Mr. T and Mr. A was very insignificant. I noticed that Mr. A did not sit. Mr. A did inform Mr. T that he was going into the conference room.

Reality began to set in that we three were the committee. I started to become very tensed, as I sat there with Mr. T and Mr. A, knowing that we were the composition of the committee. Mr. T opened his briefcase and pulled out three folders, and gave one to each of us. Inside the folder was a rough draft copy of the teachers' evaluation instrument. I looked over it very quickly without having given too much thought about the content. For a while, I had a great deal of difficulty trying to concentrate on the task at hand, due to the fact that there were only three of us present, and that I was the only individual assigned in a school, and who worked directly with the students. I began to think how unfair this designed committee and process was in regards to the other thousands of teachers in the school system. I knew that it was imperative, that I cleared any unnecessary thoughts that I was having so that I would be able to clearly focus on this evaluation instrument. The more I thought about my role as a teaching sitting with Mr. T and Mr. A, the more stressful I became, because I knew what every happened in that conference room was going to have a tremendous effect on thousands of teachers in the school system.

We began to carefully examine the teachers' evaluation instrument. We started the process by familiarizing ourselves with the entire document.

After we had read the complete document, we began to discuss in general what the outcome would have been, on adopted by the School Board. Unfortunately, I had seen may items on this instrument that would have been detrimental to teachers. In the beginning I never mentioned any of these findings. Patiently and respectfully, I remained silent to hear Mr. T and Mr. A interpretation, and what conclusion in reference to the teachers' performance outcome would have been once the instrument had been adopted by the School Board.

My interpretation of what the two males had concluded was horrifying in reference to the teachers' outcome. The instrument appeared to have been designed to further reprimand dedicated teachers in the school system. As I sat there, I thought that this instrument would help with further lowering the morals of the teachers. Teachers were already feeling that there was no hope, support, and appreciation expressed to them from anyone. Therefore, my thinking was that if the School Board adopted that instrument, this would have been the "kill" for teachers desire, enthusiasm and effort to continue.

I recall discussing certain concepts and principles that made up various performance criteria. Some of these criteria were not very clear at all, and from my interpretation as a teacher would have been just the right tool to destroy any teachers' profession. After having brought this concept to Mr. T and Mr. A's attention, both of them tried to convince me that I had misinterpreted the criteria. Although they continued to explain their rationale, I was not convinced about my feelings.

We spent the next three days going over basically the same task from the first day. In my opinion, from the results of this small committee, one day would have been sufficient. My being there was just a "ploy", because my input was meaningless. Moreover, I understood that once the School Board had adopted this instrument, they would have justified it by saying that a committee (never once identified the number of members) had made the decision, along with having a teacher representative. Again, they would have continued to use deception to the teachers and other educators. However, I was used to being deceived, and that type of behavior no longer surprised me.

The following Thursday was the regular day scheduled for the School Board Meeting. I put forth unusual effort to be present at this meeting, because I felt that the teachers' evaluation instrument was going to be one of the main items placed on the agenda for confirmation. Meanwhile, prior to the Thursday's meeting, and while back at my school, I would go to the teachers' lounge given every opportunity to inform my colleagues that a new teachers' evaluation had been written. Without letting them know that I had been a part of such, and preventing discussing other details with me, I kept my dialogue in tach, using a third person. I would say statements like, "someone had informed me that the new teachers' evaluation was going to more or less serve as a serious weapon to destroy teachers." They would not have ever dreamed that I was no longer just an attendant at the School Board Meeting, but had been chosen by the higher authorities to serve in what every capacity that they dictated.

By now, the higher authorities were comfortable with me, thus far, they had not gotten any feedback from anyone in reference to my having talked about the inside scope of the school system. The School Board Meeting for that Thursday was called to order. On the agenda, very near the end was the Teachers' Evaluation Instrument. This was included with other items that were needed to have been approved by the School Board. By the time items would reach this level, the deal was closed. Without having to pay careful attention to the board members, I knew that the teachers' troubles in the school system were yet to come. Therefore, all items were passed by all board members, without any opposition or discussion.

CHAPTER NINE

THE IMPLEMENTATION PROCESS

(The Abuse of the Teachers' Evaluation Instrument)

It was the beginning of a new school year, when I was re-assigned to my formal school. There was a new administrator, and a couple of new teachers. I recall very vividly during the first back to school faculty meeting, we were instructed upon entering into the meeting area to sign in, (something new) and to pick the items on display. Among these items were an agenda, and copies of the New Teachers' Evaluation Instrument that just included the criteria and supportive indicators in reference to the teacher's performance. I noticed my colleagues expressions as they read very quickly the information. They appeared to have been too afraid to overtly express what they were seeing. Therefore, I could only hear mumbling from the group. The teachers knew that they had to be extremely careful, because we had a new principal, and we dared not to have allowed ourselves to have gotten on his bad side the first day.

The new principal was a male. (Mr. W, I will call him) My first thought of Mr. W was who did he know in the school system to have been chosen for that position. The school that I was assigned had a reputation of having major disciplinarian problems throughout the years, and each year seemed to have gotten progressively worst. However, Mr. W appeared to have possessed all of the characteristics of masculinity to help make a positive change in the school. He was very tall, looked like he had been lifting weights, and demonstrated a no nonsense attitude. Mr. W had a baritone sounding voice that defined authority. From the very first moment that he began the faculty meeting, one could have heard a pin drop, because without having spoken it, he demanded our undivided attention. Mr. W began to share with the staff the new rules that had been implemented within the school system. He talked about the basic givens in the beginning. Nevertheless, we were sitting on the edge of our seats, waiting to get to the Teachers' Evaluation Instrument. Mr. W reminded all the teachers that they needed a copy of the evaluation to be able to follow along with him, while he reviewed it with us, adhering to the mandate that had been disseminated from headquarters. Mr. W entire tone, while going over the criteria and indicators for the teacher's performance sound more like continuous threats.

Mr. W appeared that he was going to be using this evaluation to seriously reprimand the teachers. He read each of the statements. After each statement, he would add his own interpretation, and shared with us detailed consequences should there have been any violations. He, like myself had already perceived by serving on the so-called review committee had misinterpreted the intent of many of the criteria and indicators.

I began to feel anger coming upon me. I reflected back to the three day meeting that had taken place with Mr. T and Mr. A. During this meeting, my greatest concern about how one would interpret the evaluation instrument would have been strictly judgmental. I feared this type of behavior that I was seeing in Mr. W during the entire process of having discussed the instrument prior to the School Board approval. Meanwhile, Mr. W told the staff that he would be coming into their class room unannounced, and that he was going to keep ongoing documentation of their performance. No one on the staff bothered to have commented on anything that Mr. W had shared with us. In my opinion, everyone was too afraid to do so, because Mr. W's attitude was definitely not of a friendly nature, and he expressed to us that he was there to do what he had been assigned to do.

Immediately, I made a couple of telephone calls to headquarters, inquiring about Mr. W, and why he had been sent to my school. From the sources that I contacted, I was informed that Mr. W was sent to clean house, so to speak. That meant he was to serves as an intermediator for headquarters. I continued to ask more questions about how one had concluded that he would have been the right person. Through a very reliable source, (a male) he told me that Mr. W know the prototype of the school system, and that in essence, he had passed their test. That statement aroused my curiosity even more. Therefore, this motivated me to do further investigation. When all else had been exhausted, I knew that Mr. Z was still on board, and that he would definitely share with me Mr. W's story. At this point, I contacted Mr. Z, knowing that this was fastest way to get results to my inquiry.

The next evening when I returned home from school, I called Mr. Z's private number. Mr. Z had given that number to me. He had also informed me that he was the only one who answered that number. While the phone rang, I was hoping that Mr. Z was available. After about seven rings, Mr. Z finally said hello. He appeared to have been very happy to have heard from me. We talked briefly about current issues, that I got right to the purpose of my call. I shared with him that I needed some information about Mr. W. I asked him to share with me how Mr. W got to my school. As mentioned prior, Mr. Z was heartless, and often times, behaved insensitively. Mr. Z knew that whatever he told me, that I was not going to share it with anyone. This has been confirmed and tested a couple of years ago. Mr. Z began to share with me some of Mr. W's private life styles. Everything that Mr. Z was saying was basically typical, I thought, until he said that Mr. W had done for them a favor, and to give him that promotion was his reward for the favor. Mr. Z continued to talk in details about the favor that Mr. W had done. He said that Mr. W had been involved in a sexual activity with another male who was in a top position in the state. It was because this male was sexually fulfilled, other things were done for the school system. This statement left me feeling a big numbed. I could not believe that a statue like Mr. W would have allowed himself to do such a thing to receive a promotion. Fear and disappointment saturated my mind continuously, because Mr. W had been another victim of SexCessFully Promotion.

The new school year was going along fine under Mr. W's leadership. He maintained his promise stated at the first faculty meeting. Although all of this was fine, I did not have respect for Mr. W. Therefore, it became very difficult for me to look directly at Mr. W. Every time that I was around him, all I could think about was the sexual activity that he had performed with another male just to be in that position. On some occasions, it appeared that Mr. W knew that I had found out about his behavior. I recall when he would talk to me, he seemed to have been somewhat nervous, unless, I was feeling guilty by having obtained the knowledge about his sexual activity with the other male. I must admit that I was really in a very uncomfortable position. Many times, I would wish I had not investigated how he had received the promotion. On the other hand, I was more satisfied with knowing the truth.

The end of the school year was nearing. It was evaluation time. Mr. W sent out a memo to all the staff announcing such. He had each staff member scheduled to see him privately to discuss his/her evaluation. My name had been scheduled somewhere in the middle of my colleagues. Usually, when an administrator is new, teachers who talk to him/her usually will discuss their opinion with other staff members, especially about important issues. Therefore, the teachers who had already discussed their evaluation with Mr. W seemed to have left his office very upset and angry. Most of the staff members were too afraid to virtually defend themselves. They stated to others, that it was no need to argue with Mr. W, because evaluations for teachers did not mean anything, unless one had received a rating less that satisfactory. It was no difference in treatment or respect for a teacher receiving satisfactory, good, or superior. There were no incentives for those teachers who had received superior on their performance, meeting all criteria written in the evaluation instrument.

My turn to go in to talk with Mr. W about my evaluation was coming up very quickly. I was very nervous, not because what Mr. W could have put on my evaluation, but fearing what type of behavior that I might have exemplified once into his office. Since by now, I had become that "time bomb," I could no longer trust that I could have remained calm, if I would have seen all kind of negative things on my evaluation. The time had finally arrived for me to go and meet with Mr. W. Very boldly and confidentially, I entered into his office. He was very warm and friendly. I was prepared to challenge him if my evaluation had been negative. I noticed that he did not have my evaluation on his desk. Instead of discussing my evaluation, he informed me that he had seen me on several occasions before he was assigned to the school. At that instance, my heart must have jumped several irregular beats, but still, I maintained my stamina. I politely asked him where had he seen me. His response was that he remembered me from attending the School Board Meetings. He also let me know that he knew that I knew Mr. Z and said that he would always see us laughing and talking. I did not what Mr. W was trying to find out during this dialogue. Mr. W said that he did not want to detain me any longer from my class, and that he did not have my evaluation completed, but would have it ready in a couple of days. This news was shocking, because all evaluations were completed. The deadline for the completion had arrived. Nevertheless, I did not question what he said, and politely thanked him, and left his office.

When I returned to my classroom, I could not continue to help the students, because I knew that something was not measuring up to par. I told the students that they could work on their homework. It was time that I had to go into a deep thinking process. My first thought consisted of that or worry and fear. My fear and worry were based on Mr. Z's reputation. During my thinking, I did not know if Mr. W had already concluded that I had been sexually involved with Mr. Z or what. The most stressful thing about my thinking at that moment was that I could not ask Mr. W. any further questions. Also, I did not know what Mr. Z had told him about the meetings at my house. I replayed mentally, Mr. W.s body language, while in his office. He had shown no kind of expression or indicators that would have helped with my thinking in reference to what Mr. Z had shared with him.

Time had passed for all teachers to have signed their evaluation. I knew that I had not signed mine. I had not received any correspondents from Mr. W. I began to worry. Therefore, I took it upon myself, left the classroom (after having heard Mr. W on the P.A system) and went to his office. When I arrived to his office, he looked at me in amazement. His expression showed that he was surprised that I came to his office. Without delay, I got right to the reason why I had come to his office. I recall reminding Mr.

W that I had not seen my evaluation for that school year, and asked him if he had completed it. He informed me that he was just getting ready to call me to his office to take care of this matter.

Somewhat feeling bewildered by now, I took a deep breath of relief, while Mr. W looked in a basket that was on his desk, and passed the evaluation to me. The evaluation instrument was simple. One did not have to do much thinking. The form was constructed such that at first glance, one could have determined his/her overall ratings. I noticed that Mr. W had marked all checks in my column under "superior" performance for every category. The strange thing about all of this was that he had checked superior for my attendance. During that school year, I had been absent for eight days. Satisfactory rating was five days absent. Even more surprising to me, under the comments section, he had written outstanding comments about those things that I did not do, because I had spent time reviewing the evaluation instrument at headquarters.

I was reminded after having read this of visiting a doctor's office for a regular check-up. A bill from the insurance company had been forward stating that it had been paid in full. On the invoice was listed and checked all the testes, and other procedures that were done, and in all reality, none of the tests and procedures submitted by the doctor were done. Nevertheless, I smiled as I read all of those superior comments that Mr. W had written about me. He asked if everything was all right. Without having shown over enthusiasm or appreciation for his actions, I thanked him and signed the form and left his office.

Later that day, I went to the teacher's lounge. The teachers were still discussing how unfair Mr. W had been with their evaluation. As they talked, I felt even more uncomfortable. Each teacher shared with the group his/her displeasure with Mr. W. They noticed that I had not made any comments. They asked how was my evaluation, and made reference to the fact that I had not said anything. I responded to their question very honestly, by sharing with them that I had received all superiors. My colleagues had always respected me as a superior teacher, but appeared to have been surprised that Mr. W had recognized it, because some other teachers in the lounge were also superior teachers who were not given superior ratings. Unfortunately, the other teachers did not know that I knew how Mr. W had received his promotion. It was obvious, in my opinion, why Mr. W had given me all superior ratings. Mr. W was wise enough to not have taken a chance on my having blown the whistle on him. It was very sad as I thought about my colleagues lack of knowledge about the school system, and that they were not aware that Mr. W had been SexCessFully Promoted.

The Series

(Victims of SexCessFully Promotions)

Sexual harassment, sexual activities, promotions, not promoted, reprimand, and other behavioral activities seemed to have been the way it was in the school system, according to individuals who shared their stories. I will use each story in a chapter, identifying them as series.

CHAPTER TEN

(MS. T AND MR. Y)

Ms. T (I will call her) who was a very hard working and attractive individual, and with 15 years in the school system had been assigned to a school that was very undesirable. Even though the school was undesirable, Ms. T felt like within a given time span, that she was willing to work extremely hard to implement new concepts, principles, skills, and creativity to reform the school. Ms. T knew, however that she needed the support from authorities from the headquarters. Therefore, after Ms. T had worked very tirelessly, putting a format together, she felt very confident that her plan would work in reforming the school. She knew Mr. Y, (I will call him) who was in a decision-making executive position that once if he had made a decision, it would not be questioned.

Ms. T telephoned Mr. Y, and shared with him all of the new ideas that she felt that would have helped change and improve the school. She asked for permission to come to headquarters to meet with him to share these ideas. Mr. Y, who did not know Ms. T agreed, and immediately arranged a time for the two of them to meet. Ms. T was very happy and felt that finally her hard work was getting ready to make a difference.

The day had come for the scheduled meeting. Upon arriving to Mr. Y's office, and when he first looked at Ms. T, he was in awe with her appearance. Mr. Y did not try to hide the fact that he liked her physical appearance. Ms. T said that Mr. Y told her that his office was really not a convenient place for the two of them to meet, and that he would have to re-schedule the meeting to take place other than at the headquarters. Ms. T began to wonder why all of that was necessary just to look at plans. After all, she had only wanted to share the information that she had put together to change her school, and it was nothing of a great secret about that she thought. Without going against Mr. Y's suggestions, she agreed to re-schedule the meeting. Mr. Y told Ms. T that he would call her to inform her of the place and time.

Several days had passed. Mr. Y telephoned Ms. T to inform her of the re-scheduled time for the meeting. Ms. T said that it was very strange to her where Mr. Y told her to meet him. Ms. T said that the place sound like it was a residential, and she could not figure out why a top executive would want to meet at a residential place to discuss her plans. Ms. T did not think about anything else at that time, except for making sure that she was familiar with the content that she had prepared to share with Mr. Y during the meeting.

The day of the meeting, Ms. T said that when she arrived at the address that had been given to her, it was a row house. At first, she stated that she had to double check the information, because she was having a lot of difficulty trying to figure out why that place. Ms. T stated that while feeling somewhat dismay, she played the role as if nothing was suspicious, and with unsuppressed confident, approached the house, and rang the doorbell. Mr. Y answered the door, and invited her inside. Ms. T said that it appeared that no one was at home, but Mr. Y. She said that the house did not have the atmosphere of someone really living in it. There was hardly any furniture. She remembered experiencing a feeling of emptiness upon entering. However, Ms. T said that Mr. Y appeared to have been very comfortable, and familiar with the house. Mr. Y did not offer her anything, so Ms. T concluded that it was no type of food items in the house.

Meanwhile, Ms. T said that she initiated the conversation, relating to the packet of information that she had prepared to share with Mr. Y. According to Ms. T, Mr. Y very quickly indicated to her that he was not interested in what she was saying. Instead, of listening to her, he changed the tone of the conversation. He told Ms. T that she was very attractive and sexually appealing, and therefore, he wanted to have sex with her. Ms. T said that for a moment, that statement made her speechless. She did not respond for a while. She recalled that all of a sudden, wiping perspiration from her forehead, she was feely very nervous and upset. When she finally was able to respond to Mr. Y's request, she told him no, and that she was married with children. She was not shy about letting Mr. Y know that she was faithful and respected her marriage. Mr. Y responded by informing her that she had to have sex with him in order to get his support for her concept. Ms. T still refused, and immediately left the premises.

Ms. T said that she was shocked that executive had behaved in such derogatory manner. This was her first experience with such demeanor. During the remaining of the school year, she felt ignored, a sensation of loneliness, and had zero support from the school system. She stated that she was too afraid after that encounter with Mr. Y to try another option. Therefore, she felt that she had done all of that work to help the students for nothing. Also, she shared that she could not tell anyone about this incidence, because she would have been demoted.

Ms. T underwent continuous stress, angry, and disappointment throughout the duration of the school year. She felt a relief when the end of the year was finally over. During the summer vacation, her plan was to re-group, and work on deleting any bad feelings that she had acquired during the school year. However, approximately two weeks before the opening of schools for the next school year, Ms. T received a letter from headquarters. The content of the letter was informing Ms. T that she had been transferred to another school. The school was located very far from where she lived. Needless to mention, had twice the problems of the other school. Ms. T was flawed, not having known who or where to protest this involuntary transfer. Ms. T felt hopeless, as well as helpless. She called me, and told me what had happened. She knew that I had maintained regular attendance at the School Board Meetings. Therefore, she felt that I knew someone who could have helped her.

After having received Ms. T's telephone call, I contacted Mr. Z, who was still on board. I shared with him Ms. T's story. Mr. Z said that he would get back to me after he had done some investigation. When Mr. Z returned the call, he shared with me that he had contacted Mr. Y, and that Mr. Y shared with him that the transfer should have been a warning to Ms. T for her future behavior. Mr. Z told me that Mr. Y said that transfer should have taught Ms. T a lesson. The lesson Ms. T should have learned, according to Mr. Y was not to act so high and mighty, and that if she were to succeed in the school system, she had to get off of her high horse. Moreover, Ms. T was waiting for my response to her request. It was no way that could have shared with her my findings. I told Ms. T that I was still waiting for some feedback from my inside source. Ms. T informed me that she was not going to go to the newly assigned school, and that she was going to quit education to start her own business. Because of the consequence that she had experienced, she told me she had lost respect in the total school system.

CHAPTER ELEVEN

(MS. X AND MR. C)

Ms. X, (I will call her) who was once assigned to a school, received a promotion, because of her skills and qualifications that afforded her with the opportunity to be housed at headquarters. Ms. X was making outstanding contributions to her specific assigned task, until she was selected to serve on a committee. (To prevent any finger pointing, I will not identify the committee) Ms. X was a very verbal and serious minded individual. She believed in the children, parents, and teachers in the school system. This was evident of her hard work, and the number of hours she spent helping others. Ms. X appeared to have been self-motivated, and always supporting others. In other words, Ms. X was the ideal educator.

Ms. X was not as old as most teachers who were currently in the system, and did not have many years of experience before she was promoted. This was not a problem for her, because she had earned my educational credits, attended many conferences, and thus, earned her promotion. Everything was going along very well for Ms. X, until she received a telephone call from an executive at the main headquarters. Mr. C, (I will call him) was an executive at the headquarters who had made the call. Mr. C informed Ms. X that he had seen her in the building, and wanted to invite her to his off so that he could become familiar with her duties. Ms. X said that she thought that was proper, and agreed to see Mr. C in his office at the scheduled time. Mr. C had scheduled to see Ms. X after the close of work hours. Ms. X stated that she had no problems with that, because many of the employees did not leave immediately after the end of the work day.

However, at the close of the work day, Ms. X followed the directions of Mr. C. She had no problems finding Mr. C's office. His office was located in a somewhat isolated area, away from the main flow of traffic.

Mr. C was in his office waiting for the arrival of Ms. X. Ms X stated that she never thought anything about meeting with Mr. C. She felt very comfortable and elated to have been invited by Mr. C, because she was confident with her skills and qualifications for the position of which he had been assigned. In addition, Mrs. X said that she had entertained the thought of getting to know Mr. C much better so that he would be able to help her to enhance her job performance in her position. With great enthusiasm and other pre-conceived ideas, Ms. X went directly to Mr. C's office. His door was opened. When Mr. C looked up, he invited Ms. X inside. His first statement to her was that he was glad that should make the appointment, and was hoping that she would have not forgotten.

The two of them sat in such positions where there would be full exposure of both individuals anatomy. Ms. X stated that Mr. C asked her to tell him more about herself. Like anyone else in that situation, Ms. X began to talk about her job duties, future plans, and how she planned to implement them. Ms. X said that she was so excited sharing this information with Mr. C until she was not aware that she had prolonged the dialogue. She said that she forgot to just make a brief comment and quite. After having talked for a while, she said that she noticed that Mr. C appeared to have lost interest, and became annoyed with what she was saying. However, this was the signal for her to end her dialogue. Mr. C did not respond to anything that Ms. X had said. Ms. X said that was surprising to her, because she was hoping that Mr. C would have at least suggested how he could have helped her, or created some sort of networking opportunity. Instead, Mr. C, using a very dominating type of voice told Ms. X the reason for having invited her to meet with him.

Ms. X said that Mr. C began to share with her the real reason for that meeting. Ms. X said how shocked she was when Mr. C never showed any reservations or shame when he began to tell her about the reason why she had been invited. Ms. X said that Mr. C began by telling her that she was very attractive, and sexually appealing to him, and that he was interested in pursuing a closer, non-job-related relationship. He informed Ms. X that everything that was said must be kept in strict confidence. Mr. C was at least 25 years her senior, and that she did not know how to relate to someone that old. Ms. X said that Mr. C was very close to the age of her father, and if she had gone anywhere with Mr. C, it would have been the same as being with her father.

Mr. C informed Ms. X that he was not about playing any children games, and asked her when could they get together privately, away from the headquarters. Ms. X, very stunned, as anyone could have been at her age said that she did not know exactly to respond to Mr. C's request. She stated that she did not that this type of behavior happened in the school system. She shared that she never thought about the consequences that she would have undergone by refusing to see Mr. C. privately. Ms. X stated that Mr. C demanded an answer right away. She simple told him that she could not meet with him privately. Ms. X said when she told Mr. C that, his entire mannerism changed toward her. He immediately told her in essence, to leave the office. The rest of the evening Ms. X said that for some reason, she felt uncomfortable. She could not predict what was going to happen to her after the meeting. Ms. X knew that Mr. C's comment about meeting privately meant that he wanted to have sex with her. Ms. X stated that would have been like having sex with her father.

Days passed, Ms. X said that she noticed that her sleeping and eating habits had changed. These symptoms became progressively worst as time passed, until she finally had to see a physician. The physician informed Ms. X of her prognosis that was she was suffering from a condition called manic depression that was a result of having been under severe stress. He prescribed medication for her to be treated for the condition, and asked to see her weeks later. Ms. X said that the medication had served as a temporary relief, but did not cure the stress of having to pass Mr. C in the hall while at work.

Two weeks passed, Ms. X returned t the physician for her scheduled check-up. The physician could not find any obvious change in Ms. X's condition.

Ms. X said that the physician began to ask her personal questions, and when he asked about her job, she broke down and sobbed. The physician recognized that her job was the cause of her depression. The physician asked her to describe her duties, which she did. Ms. X said that the physician had problems with trying to figure out what she had told him that would have caused such stress, because her job duties were basically typical. Ms. X was too afraid to tell the physician the real truth.

The physician scheduled to see her two weeks later. When Ms. X returned for that appointment, again there was no change in her condition. The physician counseled her, and suggested that because of her ages, skills, and qualifications she need to change jobs. Ms. X said that she did not want to change jobs, because she had been making such positive impact on the students in the school system. Nonetheless, Ms. X stated that when she arrived at work on a Friday morning and picked up her mail from her assigned mailbox, there was a business envelop inside with just her name, sealed with tape, and had stamped "confidential." Ms. X became very nervous immediately, and hurried and open the letter. The content of the letter informed her that because of her poor performance, she was going to be terminated at the end of the month. The letter was signed by Mr. C. Ms. X did not know who she could have shared this information with or even shared what had happened between her and Mr. C. She stated that if she had not had the medication, she would have easily had a nervous breakdown. Moreover, before the end of the month, Ms. X had been job hunting, and had been hired for a top position in private industry.

After having worked in her new position for a while, Ms. X stated that eventually, all of her habits had returned to normal. However, she did go back to the physician just for confirmation. When the physician gave Ms. X her final prognosis, he told her that she was fine, took her off all medication, and did not re-schedule any more appointments. Ms. X stated that was the turning point in her life, and that she was forever grateful that she did not adhere to Mr. C's request that would have made her another victim of SexCessFully Promotion just to maintain a position.

CHAPTER TWELVE

(MR. K AND MR. L)

Mr. K and Mr. L were both educators in the school system. Mr. K, however, was assigned to headquarters, and Mr. L was a classroom teacher. During that era, homosexuality was not very popular and exposed in society, like in the 90's. Therefore, when individuals would see the two of the same genders who appeared to be inseparable, no one would question sexual preference. This was the case between Mr. K and Mr. L. They were seen together at social events, etc.

As time passed, Mr. L appeared to have put some distance between himself and Mr. K. Often times, and in some instances, they would appear not to have known each other. Mr. L said that he realized that others had observed the change between the two of them, and therefore, Mr. L decided to tell his story. Mr. L stated that during the time when the two of them were going to social affairs together, that everything was based on a social and a professional relationship. Both males were married, and their wives did not want to attend some of the affairs, because it saved money on baby sitting.

Mr. L shared that while he was in the classroom, he became very tired of having to do more discipline with the students than teach his subject matter. Therefore, since he and Mr. K had become very good friends, he knew that Mr. K was in a position to help him get out of the classroom. For this reason, he decided to bring his interest of another position to Mr. K's attention. When Mr. L confronted Mr. K with the request to leave the classroom, he said that Mr. K informed him that he would have to find a position for him. Meanwhile, the two males continued being seen together. Their relationship was on just a friendship term only. Mr. K finally found a position that he felt that Mr. L would have been interested in, as well as had met the criteria for the position. Mr. K informed Mr. L of this position, and instructed him how to go about obtaining the position. Mr. L did not have any problems with adhering to Mr. K's instructions. After finalizing all requirements, Mr. L was chosen for the position.

The new position afforded Mr. L to relocate to headquarters. Mr. L was given his own office. His office was two doors down the hall from Mr. K. This allowed more time for the two gentlemen to see each other. Their friendship was still that of just good buddies. The two began to stay late at work. Instead of going directly home from work, they would stop and have drinks and sometimes dinner. These activities increased between the two, until they were hardly inseparable.

During one of Mr. K and L evenings out, Mr. K shared with Mr. L some very personal problems that he was having at home. He told Mr. L that he no longer was interested in a sexual relationship with his wife. He said that when lying in bed with her, his mind would always be on him. Mr. L replied to Mr. K's comment by sharing with him that he was not having a sexual relationship with his wife, because he had been getting home too late, and was working on plans to decrease his social activities with him, so that he could spend more time with his family. Mr. K emphatically told him how he had begun to feel about him. He stated that Mr. K told him was, and had been attracted to him sexually, and wanted to turn their friendship relationship into a sexual relationship.

Mr. L shared that neither of the two had been sexually involved with another male before. Mr. K told Mr. L although he understood that his request may have been against his morale and values, but if he were willing to give it a try, he would see to it that he would receive a substantial increase in salary. Mr. L stated that he was desperately in need for more salary. Mr. L said that he had nothing to lose, and that no would have ever found out about it, and by doing this activity, he was promised an big increase in his salary.

The two of them made arrangement to live out the planned sexual fantasy. The arrangement was that both of them would meet at a hotel very far away from the city. Each would drive his own car. Mr. K told Mr. L that he would be registering for the room, using an assumed name. Mr. L said he was comfortable with the arrangement, and followed through with the plan.

Mr. L admitted that he was excited about experimenting with the unknown. He said that he had absolutely no fear, because to his knowledge Mr. K was not a homosexual. Therefore, after whatever they would have agreed upon happened, they could continue with their lives as usual.

Plans went as arranged. Both men arrived at the hotel on time. Mr. K had ordered drinks for the room, and had requested a king-sized bed. Mr. L said that when he arrived in the hotel room, Mr. K grabbed him, and embraced him very passionately. He said that Mr. K tried to kiss him in the mouth, but politely he back away. Mr. L stated that Mr. K became erected immediately, and asked if he would perform oral sex on him. Mr. L said that he refused to do so. Moreover, Mr. L told Mr. K that he didn't mind if he would perform oral sex on him. Later on during the evening, both of them performed oral sex on each other.

After this activity, both men went home to their family. When Mr. L arrived at home, went to bed with his wife, he was feeling very guilty, but suppress that feeling by re-directing his thought to the pay raise that had been promised by Mr. K. He told his wife that he had experienced a very tiring day at work, and just did not feel like talking any more. He shared that he was working on a project that had consumed most of his time and energy, and that was the reason for not being able to be with the family like he wanted.

Back at work, and when Mr. L received the next pay, he noticed a difference in his paycheck. Mr. L said that it was $150.00 more per pay. That was a lot of money Mr. L thought just for a few moments of sexual gratification that both of them had enjoyed. Nevertheless, Mr. L thought the case had been closed, so to speak, but Mr. K asked if could see him again at another hotel. This time, with hesitation, Mr. L declined Mr. K's request. In the beginning, Mr. K did not show any type of reaction to Mr. L comment. However, Mr. L stated that after a month had passed, he received a communication from Mr. K that informed him that he was going to be transferred back to another school to assist with a newly initiative pilot program.

Mr. L confirmed that he regretted going against his morals, values, and cheating on his wife just for more money. He also stated that to add to his already existing pain, stress and shame, when he refused to have made this an ongoing activity with Mr. K, he was demoted, and there was nothing that could have done about it.

CHAPTER THIRTEEN

ACCOMPLISHING THE TASK WITH SEX

(Mr. Y and Ms. A)

Too often, individuals had to do undesirable things to please someone else. This was the situation between Mr. Y and Ms. A. Mr. Y was a very influential individual in the school system, as well as had a close relationship with some of the local Elected Officials. Ms. A was in a position that was over the local school system. Although, Ms. A was not the top chief, she was in the type of executive position that could have either helped or hurt the school system.

Mr. Y shared that his with Ms. A that was not to his willing, but was mandated that he followed directions from the people who were in higher positions. Mr. Y stated that he was instructed to improve a certain aspect in the school system. Moreover, this task would have been impossible without the assistance from Ms. A. Mr. Y shared that he did not have a direct line of communication with Ms. A, and therefore, had to use any creativity that would have opened the lines of communication, because he knew that he had to get the task accomplished.

Mr. Y carefully planned attending meetings and social affairs that he knew Ms. A would have been attendance. This was the only strategy that he could perceive that would have worked for him to be able to become familiar with Ms. A. Mr. Y stated that during an informal social affair, he found the perfect opportunity to establish the pathway to a communication line between the two of them. He recalled approaching Ms. A, complimented her, and told her that she had beautiful legs. Mr. Y appeared to have been a very cruel person. Nevertheless, Mr. Y stated that Ms. A was very unattractive person, not just in the face, but also did not have the ideal body form. Moreover, Mr. Y said that he managed to use all of his flirting tactics to obtain her telephone number. Once he would have received her number, it would have been easier for him to implement the plans that he had for Ms. A. He successfully obtained Ms. A's number. He did not call her right away, because he was trying not to blow any opportunity that would have prevented him from accomplishing his task. Nonetheless, Mr. Y knew that Ms. A was divorced. Therefore, he knew the chances for the two of them getting together were only a matter of time.

Mr. Y's time was running out to get the task done that had been demanded upon him from the higher officials. Therefore, he called Ms. A at her office. Ms. A appeared to have been very excited to have heard his voice. He said that he continued flirting with her, even during his first telephone conversation. He said to her, "how is the finest woman at the State department doing today?" Mr. Y said that Ms. A giggled like a teenager. He was convinced that by now, he had made another step toward making the next move. He said after a few minutes during the conversation, he asked Ms. A, if should would be interested in joining him for dinner the next day. Ms. A did not hesitate to accept the invitation. Mr. Y instructed Ms. A to meet him at an insignificant restaurant at specific time to avoid the regular flow of traffic that could have been individuals who would have known both of them.

Mr. Y was feeling very positive that he was well on his way to accomplishing his task. His position would have been in jeopardy, if he could not have accomplished what he had been ordered to do. However, Mr. Y shared that the only concern that he had was that, he did not know if, and when the time came that would have required a sexual activity. He was afraid that he knew it would have been very difficult for him to get an erection, because Ms. A was not appealing sexually at all, according to Mr. Y. Mr. Y stated that he became more concerned, because the only way he thought that he could have satisfied Ms. A sexually, was by performing oral sex. Mr.

Y implied that he did not believe in oral sex, and or had ever performed it before.

The next day, Ms. A and Mr. Y met at the restaurant as scheduled. Mr. Y said that Ms. A appeared a little nervous. However, Mr. Y shared that he was able to ignore her behavior, because he knew what he had to do, his position was at risk. Mr. Y stated that during the entire time while the two were having dinner, all that was on his mind was how could he ever become erected with Ms. A. He was bothered by that thought. Meanwhile, while eating, he contributed very little to the conversation. However, he had to maintain his profile that was to continue to flirt with her, by telling her how beautiful she was, and that she was one of the most appealing females at her work place. Ms. A believed Mr. Y, and by her body language, she continued to make it easy for Mr. Y to make the next move.

After dinner, the two of them left the restaurant, and went their separate way. Before the final departure, Mr. Y asked to see Ms. A on the upcoming Friday after the work hours. Ms. A appeared to have been expecting for Mr. Y to get around to asking to see her again. Mr. Y said that Ms. A with a bubbling expression all over, so to speak, mannerism, gladly agreed to meet with him. Mr. Y arranged for the two of them to meet at a not so popular hotel. Mr. Y knew that under no circumstances that he could have afforded and allowed anyone to have seen him with Ms. A.

Friday even had come faster than Mr. Y had wished. The two of them met at the hotel on time. Mr. Y did not drink alcoholic beverages, but ordered a drink anyway. He stated that he knew he had to do something drastic to help him with the situation that he was about to partake. Meanwhile, Ms. A appeared to have been very happy to have been invited to be alone with him, and upon entering into the hotel room, told him that she was going to get comfortable, and took off her clothes. Mr. Y shared that under normal conditions, he would have immediately gotten sexually aroused after a female removed her clothes, but Ms. A's body even looked worst without the clothes on. Mr. Y, very quickly started drinking the alcoholic beverage, trying to become so intoxicated so that whatever he had to do would not have mattered at that time.

Mr. Y stated that Ms. A was very aggressive after having consumed one drink. Therefore, she pursued him. Mr. Y stated that Ms. A continued with her aggressiveness, while he was having difficulty responding. He stated that usually when a female performed oral sex with a male, he would always help the male to become aroused. So he directed her to have her way, while he continued to hold back. Mr. Y was not a man of the 90's. He said that he pretended to have gone to the bathroom, instead he went to the dresser where the alcoholic beverages were, and drank almost a half of glass straight. He shared that when he returned back to the bed with Ms. A, he was very intoxicated, and began to perform oral sex on her. He shared that he hated having to violate his principles, but all he could think about at the moment was hold onto his position. Mr. Y tried to last about ten minutes and stopped, got dressed and insisted that Ms. A dressed as well. After having dressed, Mr. Y asked Ms. A if he could stay for a while longer, because there was something he wanted to discuss. Ms. A adhered to this this request. Mr. Y said that while both of them were still in the frame of mind of somewhat intoxicated, he informed Ms. A that her assistance was needed to accomplish his assigned task. Without any reservation, Ms. A promised Mr. Y that she would take care of his request, and assured him that everything would be all right.

A few days had passed when Mr. Y received a communication from Ms. A that confirmed that his request had been approved. Mr. Y immediately shared this information with the higher official. The higher official showed sincere appreciation to Mr. Y for having accomplished the assigned task. Mr. Y, on the other hand, said that he was very pleased, because he did not have to worry about staying in his position. However, he knew that he had violated his principles, morals, and values just to keep such position. He said that from time-to-time, Ms. A would call his office, but he had informed his secretary to always was tell her that he was out of the office, and would get back to her. After Ms. Had called so much, she realized that Mr. Y was really not interested in her, and therefore, Ms. A must have felt that she had experienced a SexCessFully endeavor.

CHAPTER FOURTEEN

FROM CLASSROOM TEACHER, DIRECTLY TO PRINCIPAL

(Ms. R and Mr. M)

Ms. R had been teaching in the school system for about six years before she met Mr. M. Mr. M was in a higher position, whereas, he could make decisions for individuals in the school system that no one would have questioned. Ms. R was in her late 20's at the time, and Mr. M was in his early 50's. Ms. R was a very attractive, shapely, and had family members in what we could call "high" places. I must mention that Mr. M had once been a member of the group that met at my house during the earlier years. Mr. M knew that by now, no one had talked about previous sexual activities, and he felt safe continuing the behavior. Meanwhile, Mr. M had to visit Ms. R's school by request from the higher officials in the school system. Ms. R shared that she recalled having to go to the main office in her school to meet with a parent. At that time, a very well-dressed distinguished looking gentleman spoke to her. Ms. R said that the gentleman seemed to have come from out of nowhere. However, Ms. R did not think anything about the gentleman in the building, because in her school, it was not unusual to see visitors at any given time in the building. Nevertheless, Ms. R said that when she had finished meeting with the parent, she left the principal's office. Directly outside of the office door was the same gentleman who had spoken to her before she met with the parent. She said that this gentleman appeared to have been deliberately waiting for her. After Ms. R came out of the office, the gentleman, once again spoke to her and introduced himself. He told her he as Mr. M, and proceeded to tell her about the position that he held, while indicating that he could help her.

Ms. R recalled Mr. M starring at her in a very unusual manner, while he was talking to her. She said at that particular time, Mr. M did not give her any indication that he was interested in her sexually. She said if he had shown such, because of her age, and lacking in experience of how some people behaved in the school system, that she would have never believed it anyway. Ms. R like most young women at her age could not perceive someone in Mr. M's position spending any type of social time with her. One must reflect back and remember, during that era in education, a "big chief" would have dared to be seen socializing with a classroom teacher. However, Ms. R said that she felt flattered that Mr. M thought that she was at least worthy of his speaking to her. Ms. R soon forgot that incident.

Weeks had passed, Ms. R was in the midst of one of her daily lessons, the PA system clicked. It was the principal paging her to come immediately to the office, because she had received a very important telephone call. Ms. R stopped in the middle of her lesson, and went directly to the main office. While walking down the hall to the main office, Ms. R said that she tried to imagine who was so important to have called her at school, and that caused the principal to respond so quickly. When Ms. R arrived in the main office, the secretary directed her to the telephone line where the caller was waiting. Ms. R was a bit nervous. She said "hello," a voice responded by identifying himself right away. He replied by saying, "this is Mr. M, remember I met you at your school a couple of weeks ago by the main office?" Ms. R had no problem with remembering having met Mr. M. After all, she said that Mr. M had been the first "high" official that she had met during her six year tenure. Out of shock, Ms. R said that it appeared that she was standing there speechless. Ms. R stated that Mr. M got straight to the purpose of his call, which was to get her home telephone number. He told her that he needed her number, because someone had told him about her qualifications and skills, and that he would like to meet with her to discuss further how they could best utilized such in the school system. On her way back to her classroom, all she could think about was that she was going to be getting a pay raise.

Exactly two days had passed when her telephone rang at home at 7:00 p.m., and the called was Mr. M. Mr. M, according to Ms. R was a very direct type of person. She said that he waste no time getting to the point of this matter. Ms. R stated that without prolonging any sort of dialogue, Mr. M informed her that he would like to meet with her the upcoming Thursday of the next week. He continued to give her complete directions as to where he had planned for them to meet. Ms. R said that she was not familiar with the area, but knew that would not been a problem locating the house. The house was at my house. As mentioned prior, Mr. M was aware that I lived alone, and had an empty apartment. He knew that other activities had occurred at my house, and that no one knew about them, except for the participants. Therefore, he trusted that I would still remain silent. Mr. M called me, and asked if he could meet someone at my house for about an hour. I admit that I was anxiously awaiting to see who had been chosen to see.

Thursday arrived without my having concentrated on the planned coming even. By now, I no longer believed in fairness of individuals in "key" positions in the school system, because I had seen too much wrong doing. I was already convinced that nothing else could have surprised me. Therefore, it did not matter to me what was going on. All I knew, I was going to maintain my position, and that I was not going to allow myself to become SexCessFully Promoted. Nonetheless, the doorbell rang, and standing at the door was a very attractive young lady who looked much young than her actual age. She introduced herself as Ms. R, and shared that she had been directed to meet Mr. M at my address. I invited her in, and found out more about her. All the time that we talked, I could hardly help but ask myself, "why would such a beautiful you lady allow herself to be manipulated by some higher official?"

Very shortly after the arrival of Ms. R, Mr. M arrived. In his usual manner, Mr. M invited Ms. R to my empty apartment. They stayed in the apartment for about three hours. At one time, I began to worry, because most of the time that they were there, I heard no sounds. Moreover, the sounds that I heard appeared to have been body contacts, not too much verbal interaction. Finally, both of them came to my apartment. They did not have too much to say. Both thanked me, and returned to their cars and left. I noticed that Ms. R was driving a luxury car. I didn't think anything about that, however, because Ms. R had already told me that she was single, no children, and lived with her parents. Ms. R, and nor Mr. M showed no remorse for having participated in the suspected sexual activity. Ms. R kept in touch with me, by calling from time-to-time. She was not seeing Mr. M that regularly, but did admit to seeing him occasionally. The two were meeting at different hotels.

The school year had come to an end. Everyone was happy as always to end another school year. Ms. R had not gotten an increase in her salary as expected. She began to worry about what Mr. M had in mind for her, because she knew that something had to be forthcoming, because of her sexual involvement with him. She said that about three weeks after schools had closed, that she received a memorandum from the headquarters. The memorandum informed her that she had been selected to come in for an interview for a principal's position.

Regardless, to Ms. R's conviction, she adhered to the directive, and showed up for the interview. Ms. R said that the interviewing panel consisted of four individuals, one female and three males. One of whom was Mr. M, who was also the other three panelists superior. Ms. R said that Mr. M directed the interview. He started the interview by telling the other panelists how successful she had been during her six year tenure in education. He continued by making up contributions about what Ms. R had done within the school system. Ms. R said that while Mr. M shared this information with the panelists, she was in total disbelief, because she knew that she had never done anything that caused her to receive any kind of attention. Ms. R said that the other panel members hardly had anything to say during the interview. She stated that she was very bewildered the entire time during the interview. At the conclusion of the interview, Mr. M implied that Ms. R would be able to perform as an excellent principal, while reminding the panel that excellent principals were needed very badly in the school system.

One week later, Ms. R said that she received a letter in the mail in an official envelop from the school system's personnel department. When she opened and read the letter, it clearly stated, beginning with congratulation, and further informing her that she had been selected to be the new principal at School X, beginning immediately. Ms. R said that she almost underwent a panic attack, because she did not expect to have received that type of information. She also stated that she felt very incompetent in the beginning, because she knew that she had not taken the courses that were pre-requisites that would have enhanced her skills and knowledge as a principal. However, Ms. R accepted the position, and begun her duties immediately in the capacity of a principal.

Nevertheless, Ms. R said that it was not the end of Mr. M and their relationship. She shared that Mr. M clearly defined what her future role was going to be, once having received principal's salary. He told her that her other responsibility was to purchase his clothing items, i.e. suits, shirts and ties on occasion, as well as other items such as his favorite cologne. Ms. R said that she could not have refused his request, because she felt that she had fallen too deeply into the undercover trap of things. Instead, she did not have any other choice, but to adhere to his request. Ms. R stated that she bought Mr. M several clothing items at his request for at least the next three years. Ms. R said that often times, she felt very embarrassed, and not worthy of her position, because it was just another SexCessFully Promotion.

CHAPTER FIFTEEN

THE ELECTED OFFICIAL AND THE PRINCIPAL

(Ms. P and Mr. Q)

Ms. P was a principal in the school system. Ms. P had served in that position for three years prior to meeting Mr. Q. Mr. Q held a very impressive title in a neighboring county. Ms. P shared in her story by letting it be known, that she did not like being a principal in the school system. She felt that she never received the adequate support from the headquarters. Needless to mention, the lacking of support from the parents of the children, not having enough staff members for the student enrollment, as well as having to undergo ongoing disciplinarian problems, and having to listen to continuous teachers distress and complaints. Therefore, Ms. P classified her position as a principal as the worst job that she had ever experienced.

Ms. P was continuously under scrutiny for the performance of the students who attended her assigned school. In every category on the standardized tests, her school rated among the lowest of all the other schools. She said that there was no stability with the staffing. At the end of each school year, many of the teachers would put in for a volunteer transfer, and that these would always be the teachers who were among the best in the school. In return, she said that it appeared that the system would always replace these good teachers with teachers who were incompetent and not even state certified. She shared that there were not enough teachers assigned to her school in relationship to the student body. Therefore, class sizes were much too large, thus, this created severe disciplinary problems.

In the beginning, she thought that this trend was only going to be temporary. However, each year, according to Ms. P matters became progressively worst. Ms. P said that she had become overwhelmed with stress, needless to mention, was feeling a sensation that she was continued to have been ignored by the executives at headquarters. She shared that she felt that she was stuck in a "no-win" situation, because in order to move ahead in her career, she knew that she needed a doctorate, which she did not have. She could not afford to go back to school to earn another degree, because she was married, with small children. After a day's work at her school, and having to take care of family matters, she was too exhausted for anything else.

Ms. P recalled, while out to dinner after a meeting that had taken place at headquarters, and while there, the top executive from the neighboring county came over to her table and introduced himself. Everyone at the table knew Mr. Q, because of his position, but that had never met him personally. Also at the dinner table were three other females. Ms. P said that Mr. Q gave each of the ladies one of his executive cards, and departed. Meanwhile, Ms. P dreaded gong to her school continuously. She stated that each day in her school was becoming even more depressing. She recalled experiencing an instant thought, and that was to contact Mr. Q, and perhaps maybe he could have helped her, or at least have shared with her more directions in reference to how she could get out of the school system.

Ms. P said that she had developed enough courage to go into her office, and call Mr. Q. She shared that his personal secretary answered the call, and like others in the same position, she demonstrated excellent skills in screening his calls. Ms. P stated that for her not having a "just" cause for calling, she told the secretary that he was expecting a call from her. Mr. Q suddenly picked up call in his private office. She said that she knew that was alone, and because of desperation, she didn't try to cover up too much. She said that she shared with Mr. Q her frustration, the lacking of support from the school system, and that she was interested in re-locating to the county.

Mr. Q appeared to have perceived what Ms. P was saying very well. He did not immediately make any promises. Instead, he asked if he could meet with her. He shared with her that he was a life-long member of a private club, and asked Ms. P to meet him there. Ms. P said that she did not hesitate at all by saying yes to his invitation. Mr. Q said he had scheduled a meeting out-of-town, and that he would be able to meet with her within the next two weeks, and thus, made an arrangement to meet with her at that time. Ms. P stated that the arrangement for her was excellent. This arrangement allowed for more time for her to come up with the most meaningful concepts to discuss with Mr. Q during the scheduled meeting. She said that when she called Mr. Q. she was so disgusted with the school system until she did not have anything on her mind specifically in reference to the type of position that shew as seeking in the county. All she knew that anything would have been much better than being in her current position. She shared that if Mr. Q had been willing to help her, she already knew that there was going to be a price to pay. Ms. P had already paid a sexual price to have obtained her current position. Therefore, she said that just to be engaged sexually would not have any bearings on her morals and values.

Two weeks passed, the day before the scheduled meeting between Ms. P and Mr. Q, the telephone rang in her office. Her secretary informed her that it was Mr. Q's secretary on the line, waiting to speak with her. Ms. P said that she had no other choice, but to be calm when her secretary gave her this information. Ms. P shared that she took a deep breath before picking up the receiver, and by using the most professional tone of behavior answered and identified herself. Mr. Q's secretary informed her that she was calling for Mr. Q who was waiting to speak with her. Ms. P stated that it took Mr. Q about two minutes before he picked up the phone. She said that the waiting time gave her more time to collect her thoughts. Mr. Q's first statement to Ms. P was an apology for having her to wait. He continued the conversation by sharing with her how busy his day had been. However, he reminded and confirmed the scheduled meeting that had been planned for the next day. Ms. P shared that during the rest of the school day and all that night, she was very nervous. She missed another scheduled meeting that afternoon, because of the anticipation of the next day's meeting.

Ms. P did not know exactly what she was going to ask Mr. Q. However, she said that she always believed that when a female projected her sexual attributes to a male that almost, always, that allowed the female to be psychologically in control of the situation. Therefore, with this in mind, her first and foremost concern was to make sure that she wore something that would have been very sexually appealing. Ms. P purchased the right type of outfit to meet her goal. She recalled buying a very clingly red knit dress that had a V-neck line that would show some cleavage. She had practiced at home while sitting, slightly bending forward, until she was satisfied that would have captured Mr. Q's attention without a doubt. Ms. P did not have professional plan to discuss with Mr. Q, she felt that her sexual oriented physical plan was sufficient.

The two days had arrived for the scheduled meeting between Ms. P and Mr. Q. When Ms. P arrived at the private club, Mr. Q was sitting at a table somewhat isolated. She shared that she was very nervous, but felt confident that Mr. Q would have been so overwhelmed with her sexiness until nothing else would have mattered. As she approached Mr. Q's table, he was pre-occupied with papers that he had taken from his briefcase, and did not look up and see her until she was standing right at the table. He looked up and saw her, and appeared to have been overwhelmed with her dress attire. Mr. Q had only seen Ms. P in a business suit, and by surprised his nervousness caused him to spill his coffee. Ms. P knew she had his attention, so she exaggerated her sitting down, and continued with this behavior throughout the meeting. She was feeling great by now, and was no long nervous, because everything seemed to have been reversed. Ms. P was definitely in control of the conversation, and continued to lean slightly over the table to remind Mr. Q that the V-neck was there, when she felt that she was losing control of the conversation.

Meanwhile, Ms. P shared that during the dialogue, and because Mr. Q was so excited, they did not get very much accomplished. The only lead that came from that meeting was that Mr. Q asked her if she had earned a doctorate, and Ms. P had not. Mr. Q informed her that he had an executive position that he could fill immediately, but the position required someone with a doctorate. Mr. Q asked Ms. P if she were interested in receiving a doctorate. Ms. P's response was yes, but could not afford the finance, or the time to do so. Mr. Q told Ms. P that he did not foresee that as a problem, because he knew the right individual at a university who would take care of her needs. H promised her that he would make all the necessary arrangement for her to enter and finish the doctoral program with his friend as her mentor at the university. Meanwhile, Mr. Q told Ms. P that because of the time, he had to go home. He needed to spend some time with his wife and children. Before they departed, he asked her to meet with him soon, and that he would contact her to schedule the date and time.

Ms. P said that when they departed, she never had felt so relieved, because she knew that she had turned Mr. Q on sexually, and that he was going to make every effort to help her get away from the school system. During the next several days, Ms. P was anxiously awaiting to hear from Mr. Q. She shared that Mr. Q was a very sexually appealing male, and if nothing would have happened in reference to her leaving the school system just to have been involved with him sexually would have pleased her.

After one week had passed, Ms. P received a telephone call. Again, it was Mr. Q's secretary calling for her for him. Ms. P was confident that this was a call to meet for a sexual affair. Mr. Q seemed to have been busy, and did not have very long for a dialogue. He got right to the point and scheduled a meeting place and time with Ms. P. The place was at a hotel. She said the most confusing part about the hotel was that it was not in isolation, or was it in Mr. Q's county.

Before that meeting, Ms. P went shopping again. This time was to purchase some very sexy exotic lingerie. She chose "red" because of her hair color. Ms. P was so confident that the lingerie would be exactly what Mr. Q would have responded to immediately. She paid far too much money for it. She said that she did not mind paying the price, because what she had planned to in the long run. Ms. P could not take the lingerie into her house, because her husband could have seen it. If he would have seen the lingerie, he would have known that was out of character for her, so she left it in the trunk of her car until the time for her to meet Mr. Q.

Ms. P arrived at the hotel earlier than the schedule time, went into the bathroom to change into the new lingerie. She sat in the lobby of the hotel (wearing a coat) until Mr. Q arrived. Finally, Mr. Q arrived. The room was already confirmed. Both pretended that they did not know each other. Mr. Q picked up the room key, and proceeded to the assigned room. Ms. P waited for about ten minutes when there was less traffic in the main lobby to proceed to the room. Mr. Q had ordered ha high quality wine by the time Ms. P arrived to the room. She recalled that the room had an almost perfect atmosphere for the activity that was about to happen. Upon entering the room, Mr. Q greeted her with a passionate embrace. He told her that he had been having sleepless nights thinking about the opportunity to see her. Mr. Q lost no time asking Ms. P to get comfortable. Ms. P undressed in front of Mr. Q by just removing her top coat. She was wearing a red robe, and beneath such was a red laced bra and matching panties. The Moment Mr. Q saw the red underwear, he became sexually aroused instantly. Ms. P stated that Mr. Q make her feel very special and appreciated, instead of treating her like a stranger in bed, she felt she had known him for a very long time. Both spent six hours in the hotel room. Ms. P shared that for a first time sexual affair, she felt very close to Mr. Q, and also felt that he was just not another executive who was using her sexually.

After their sexual encounter, they began to talk. Although, both were very fond of each other, she did not lose focus. Mr. Q told her that he had contacted the university's top authorities, and they had confirmed that Ms. P could just walk directly into their doctoral program. The made special provisions such that all of the expense would be paid, as well as not having to spend much time away from her family while taking the required classes. Mr. told Ms. P that he would obtain the necessary documents from the school, and forward them to her. Ms. P's directions were to give the documents back to Mr. Q, and Mr. Q would hand-deliver them to the authorities at the university so that everything would look official.

School had closed for the summer vacation, and Ms. P started the doctoral program. Mr. Q had made arrangements for Ms. P to meet with the decision-making authorities from the university, approximately three weeks after her enrollment. The meeting had been arranged to be very private. During the meeting, Mr. Q and the top authority shared with Ms. P that everything would just be fine during her tenure at the university, and that by the end of the following year, she would receive a doctorate. Ms. P did not understand how she would have obtained a doctorate that fast. However, she did not question the two authorities, because after all, they were the top decision-makers.

During the entire year, while attending the university, she hardly attended class, as well as did not understand the subject matter. She had missed many assignments and required testes. Also during that time, she and Mr. Q were sexually intimate on an average of once a week. She shared with Mr. Q that she was afraid that she would not be able to fulfill the university's requirements for her doctorate. All the while, Mr. Q kept telling her not to worry, and that everything would be just fine.

Graduation time was approaching, and Ms. P had made very poor grades, and in all reality, had not done her research for her dissertation, needless to mention, did not know what her grades were that were recorded. She had never received a grade report since her enrollment. Therefore, she was convinced that she would not have received a doctorate during the upcoming graduation. Moreover, shortly before graduation, she recalled receiving a letter from the university. The content of the letter began by congratulating her on having met all of the requirements to receive her doctorate at the upcoming graduation exercises. Ms. P was so bewildered until she was too afraid to broadcast the news. However, she had to share the news with her husband. She said that her husband did not know any better, because he was a blue-collar worker, and did not understand too much about the operation of colleges and universities.

Ms. P's husband expressed sincere gratitude, and told her that she had certainly worked very hard for the degree. Ms. P's husband made mention of the many days and evenings that she had spent working her degree, and that she most definitely deserved it. Ms. P's husband never had a "clue" that she was spending that time with Mr. Q, or did he suspect that Ms. P very rarely had gone to school. Although, Ms. P never studied at home, or did any type of school work, he never questioned her. Often times, she would tell her husband that she did her school work back at school in her office, and that was why she could not come home early, and adhere to a wife's schedule. Ms. P's husband would always appear to be most grateful, while taking on her chores at home. Ms. P shared that if she had not been so frustrated and disgusted with the school system, she would have felt very badly when her husband had taken on all the house chores, as well as demonstrated the feeling of how proud he was with her accomplishment. Fortunately, she said that she did not feel guilty, because of desperation, she did not entertain the thought of such, and that all she wanted to do was to leave the school system.

Finally, graduation had arrived. Ms. P participated in all of the "pre and "post" activities that usually are part of graduation. She remembered when they called her name, and awarded her with the degree, she was so pre-occupied with the thoughts of what was the next move for her. She stated that many questions were on her mind, such as how much longer would she and Mr. Q would be sexually involved, and if she were going to be leaving the school system. Mr. Q did not attend the graduation.

Ms. P telephoned Mr. Q after a week had passed to thank him for everything that he had done to make it possible for her to receive a doctorate. Mr. Q requested to meet with her about three day after that call. Once again, they met privately, and were sexually involved. After the sexual activity, Mr. Q shared with Ms. P that he had been in the process of securing a top state position for her. Mr. Q told her that everything should be confirmed by the end of that week, and that she would be getting a letter from the personnel officer relating this information to her. Sure enough, Ms. P recalled that on a Saturday, in the mail was a letter from the State's Personnel Department. She hurriedly opened the envelope, and the content stated that she had been selected to head a very significant program, and offered her the options as to when she would like to begin her new post.

Ms. P followed the proper protocol, and sent a resignation letter to the school system expressing great enthusiasm and joy of having served. She started her new post immediately after she resigned from the school system.

Dr. Estella Ingram-Levy

Ms. P said that because of her continuous stress, angry, depression and the lacking of support from the school system, she never regretted becoming SexCessFully Promoted. Ms. P continued to see Mr. Q, and eventually divorced her husband. Mr. Q did not divorce his wife. Their relationship last approximately two years before it was terminated.

CHAPTER SIXTEEN

THE NEXT DECADE

Another decade had passed, and there was still no obvious hoe for me in the school system. I still maintained my morals and values, and refused to have become SexCessFully Promoted. It seemed like SexCessFully Promotions, or serious sexual harassment was on the up-rise. I was convinced that no matter how much I would have accomplished, I would always recall the original expression from the Commissioner, and that was, "until you learn how to drop your draws, you will never receive a promotion, and that life for you in this system is going to be unpleasant and difficult for you."

It had been a while since I had received any college credits. I thought that perhaps, if I would return to school, and take administrative courses, there would have been nothing that would have prevented me from receiving a promotion. Although, I had taken many workshops, attended conferences continuously, not just inclusively geared toward my discipline, but had obtained other concepts and principles that were generic, and would have provided the qualifications for most advertised positions in the school system. Nevertheless, the following summer after the closing of school, I enrolled at Johns Hopkins University. My major was Administration and Supervision. I began to feel much better about having enrolled in school, and taking qualifying courses so that in the future, there would not have been any excuse used that would have prevented me from receiving a promotion. Moreover, and not having to have sex like many educators whom I knew had done for their promotions.

Actually, I loved and enjoyed taking the various Administrative courses. My grades were all A's in the courses. I took courses that were geared toward certain positions. Although, the courses were basically common sense, I knew that society was based on what was on paper. Therefore, I continued to take courses until I had acquired 18 credits in Administration and Supervision. I had already received my Master's Degree, plus other credits. I received my Master's two years after I had started my teaching career. However, My Master's was in my discipline which was science.

Nonetheless, there were many advertisements posted on bulletin boards in the schools continuously that related to many of the qualifications that I had obtained. As mentioned prior, I was feeling very confident that once having applied for one of the advertised positions at that time, there would not have been a problem academically in reference to not having met the advertised criteria. The announcements of the positions would always indicate the need for fulfillment immediately. All of the announcements included the criteria that were needed in reference to experience and education. Also included, were responsibilities and duties for the positions. I had no fear of not having met the advertised criteria. By this time in my career, I had gained a surmountable amount of experience, because of the many conferences and ongoing workshops that I had attended to keep up with the current trends in education. It appeared that I was among the top 10 percent of the teachers in the school system that adhered to continuous educational training. Most teachers would often time express the fact, that to attend conferences and workshops were too time consuming, as well as too costly. Many teachers felt that after having learned many new skills, it would have been very difficult to return to their assigned schools to implement them with their students. This training required up-dating equipment, and lowering class sizes. All of us knew by having been in the school system for a while, that the funds were not going to be allocated to the individual schools to make this type of improvement in the school system. In other words, teachers had adopted the feeling of hopelessness.

I recall while reading the various type of advertised positions, that one of them in particularly, was what I thought I wanted to do as a change from the classroom. Therefore, I copied all the information needed, called for the application, and followed the direction. I was able to meet the closing deadline. After several days, I received a post card from headquarters that informed me that they had received my packet. I began to feel much better by having received that acknowledgement. Many of my colleagues in the past had stated that they had applied for various positions, and had ever received any type of acknowledgement of any kind. Therefore, I felt that the system was finally making a turnaround, and that things were going to be getting progressively better for everyone, especially the teachers.

A couple of weeks passed, I had not received any further information from headquarters in reference to the position of which I had applied. I began to become somewhat curious. I called the contact person whose name was on the application. The contact person informed me that she was in the process of contacting the applicants to schedule an interview. She also said that the process would only take about three days, and that we should receive a notice in the mail thereafter. She informed me that once having received the notice, there would be further instructions. Meanwhile, I could not tell anyone that I had applied for the position. I had learned a long time ago, that I could not trust individuals in the school system. The feeling that I had while waiting to hear from the contact lady was one of nonchalant. Although, I wanted the position, and had met all the necessary qualifications to be selected for the position, I still remained calmed. I had learned enough about the school system by now not to have become very excited about anything, because of the consequences that other educators whom I knew had already undergone to obtain their positions. Because I knew that, I had no plan in changing my belief about SexCessFully Promotions. I avoided all of the pre-conceived thoughts of being able to be selected for the position without having been involved with a sexual activity.

In a couple of days, after having returned home from my assigned school, there was a letter in my mailbox from headquarters. Before opening the letter, I suspected that it was the announcement about when to come in for an interview. I recall very clearly, the letter informed me that I had been scheduled to meet at headquarters for an interview at 1:30 p.m. on the upcoming Tuesday. I knew that I had to miss going to my school, and take a sick leave day to meet the appointment scheduled for that time. My school did not let out until 3:00 p.m. I could not come up with a legitimate excuse to tell my principal that I had been scheduled for an interview at headquarters. Again, no one appeared to have been able to trust anyone. I suspected if I had told my principal, and asked him for a favor to let me take off a little earlier that day, he would have contacted someone at headquarters. Thus, this was how the games were played in the school system. There was always someone going behind an individual's back to either hurt or help a person.

The day of the interview, I stayed home from work so that I would be fresh in appearance, as well as in thought. I arrived at the headquarters about 20 minutes before my scheduled appointment. In the waiting area, were three more applicants waiting to be interviewed for the same position. Inside the board room was an applicant being interviewed. While waiting, the four of us talked among ourselves. My purpose for having initiated the conversation between the other applicants was to find out where, perhaps, I stood in reference to having been selected for the position. During our dialogue, and after having listened to each applicant share his/her qualifications, I was even more convinced that I was going to be more likely selected for the position.

The applicant, who was being interviewed upon my arrival, finally had completed the interview. When he left the office, he told us that interviewing panel told him not to discuss any of the questions that he had been asked with the waiting applicants. Therefore, he said very little. He did tell us, however that there were ten questions on the board that we had to answer. He would not tell us what any of the questions were about.

It was my turn to into the board room. The moderator asked if I would sit at the head of the table. Seated around the table were twelve people. Before the interview started, each person introduced himself/herself, and gave a brief synopsis of his/her background. The moderator shared with the group the information about me that included my skills, qualifications, and experience. In my opinion, she appeared to have subtly directed the panelist to select me for the position. She kept emphasizing that I was most qualified. It was because of her positive and supportive attitude that she had exemplified toward me, I felt very comfortable and relaxed before attempting to respond to the first question.

The moderator started the interview by having me to read alone, while she read aloud the ten questions that had been written on a chalk board. She explained why each question had been included for the interview. I noticed that each panelist had a sheet of paper in front of him/her. The paper appeared to have had some type of scoring categories. As I would finish responding to a question, each panelist would take about two minutes to rate my response. Since I was seated at the head of the table, I could see a lot of the panelist paper, and could see how each scored. I saw a 100% of them scoring the high category. Therefore, after I had completed responding to all of the statements were on the board, I felt that I would have been receiving a confirmation that would have informed me that I had been selected for the position. Each panel member appeared to have been very impressed with me in general. They made such positive comments, expressed their appreciation, and not yet, spoken confirmation. Before I l left the room, the moderator thanked me for coming, and informed me that I would be hearing from her very shortly. All the while that she was commending my performance, I noticed a very positive glow with her attitude, she was smiling the entire time.

When I left the headquarters, I was feeling exceptionally well. My thoughts were that, at last I will be able to witness fairness in the school system. I was convincing myself that SexCessFully Promotions were, perhaps something that was a thing of the past, and that I would be finally set free from always having to worry about having to have sex to receive a position.

Back at my assigned school, I was beginning to feel like I had once felt when I did not know about SexCessFully Promotions. I was not experiencing very much stress and anger anymore. I was beginning to re-think my opinion about justice in the school system. I was somewhat feeling so free, until I recall being more creative, innovative and concerned for my students. Once again, I began to implement new ideas, principles, concepts and applications with my subject matter. All the time during my severe stressful time I had not stopped attending conferences and workshops. I had kept up with the new trends that were geared toward education, but I did not have the energy or the willingness to integrate any of this with my students. My mind stayed too pre-occupied with worries.

Exactly five days after I had been interviewed, I received a letter from headquarters. Someone had sent the letter to my school. I felt that this could have been dangerous, because I did not want anyone to know that I had applied for the position, especially my principal. I did not open the letter until I was alone. When I opened the letter, instead of congratulating me for have been selected for the position, the letter's opening was, "I regret to inform you that you were not selected for the position." The remaining content of the letter wished me good luck and success in seeking a promotion, the standard jargon included in most form letters. At that moment, after having read that letter, I recall having a sincere setback. I knew that something had happened to block my having been selected for that position. I knew that I had met all required criteria for the position, and had the documents on file to have proven it. However, the only recourse that I had was to contact the individual who had served as the moderator during the interview.

I telephoned her office, it about ten minutes before she answered my call. This waiting period did not matter to me, because I was that determined to speak with her. When she finally answered, I did not hesitate to share with her my reason for calling, and requested an explanation as to why I did not receive the promotion. I requested to see a copy of the evaluation from the interviewing panel. She told me that request was against the school system's police to share that type of information. I thought that was very strange, because in all fairness, one should have been allowed to review, and discuss any matter that was pertaining toward his/her involvement. Although, her response temporarily had seemed to have caused my thinking to freeze, I felt somewhat helpless by not having known what steps to take immediately.

I spent the next several days trying to process a list of individuals who I could call at the headquarters so that I could have been given some sort of satisfactory explanation, particularly, after having done so well on the interview, and having met all required criteria for the position. However, just before the scheduled School Board Meeting, and while there I asked some of the top officials about the process of how one could retrieve personal information without having to worry about "rubbing" someone the wrong way, so to speak. I followed my intuition, and attended the scheduled School Board Meeting. During the school Board Meeting, I hardly paid any attention to the evening's agenda. My mind was too pre-occupied with trying to figure out who I should have asked to share with me further direction on how to obtain the information that I needed. As I observed all of the top officials in attendance, I was able to narrow my contact persons down to three. I must mention these were the individuals who I have become comfortable with approaching.

After the School Board Meeting had adjourned, I did not waste any time approaching the final three officials that I had pre-selected to help me. Two of them behaved in somewhat a non-caring manner, and did not give any positive directions. While the remaining gentleman gave enough information for me to feel like I had made at least a step forward. He was Mr. A. (I will call him) Mr. A was an executive, and because of his position, he had access to everything at headquarters. Mr. A appeared to have been in a hurry to leave the premise, but did ask if I would call him for further directions.

The next day, I called Mr. A and reminded him that he had invited me to call him. He had no problems in remembering our brief conversation. I told Mr. A in details what had happened. I shared with him that I had seen the panel members checking off all outstanding ratings in the category that rated the results of the interview. He appeared to have been listening very attentively. He was very patience. After I had finished with the explanation, he told me that he had to check on some things, and asked if I would call back in a couple of days.

I waited about a week before I called Mr. A. During this conversation, Mr. A said that he had been in contact with Mr. Z (The School Board Commissioner). Mr. Z was the Chairperson of the Selection Committee that confirmed this type of appointment. Mr. A shared that Mr. Z put him on hold, while he looked at my files. Mr. Z told him that I had received all unsatisfactory ratings on my interview. Mr. Z shared that on paper I had met all of the required criteria for the position, but could not confirm the position for me, because of the interview score. Meanwhile, he was one of the panelist who had served on the interview, and had a brief conversation. I asked him how had I done on the interview. He responded with overwhelming enthusiasm, and told me that all of them had rated me a 100% in all of the outstanding categories. He continued to share with me that all of the panel members agreed without having any opposition, that I had been selected for the position. I did not share with him that I had received a rejection letter.

Mr. Z and Mr. A had the type of relationship that each of them felt comfortable enough to express his uncensored feelings. Therefore, Mr. A said that Mr. Z very blatantly told him that he would have ever confirmed anything for me. Although Mr. Z did not call my name, he, instead referred to me using the "B" word. Mr. A said that Mr. Z told him that because of my attitude, he had planned to black everything that I tried to do. Mr. Z was the individual who had told me very early in my teaching career, that I didn't learn how to drop my draws, I would never get anywhere in the school system, and that life would be very difficult for me.

Mr. A knew and trusted me well enough to have shared exactly what Mr. Z had said. He also knew that by having shared this information with me, he would not have undergone any type of consequences, because if I had told anyone, no one would have believed me, because I was a classroom teach. Classroom teachers, in my opinion, were synonymous with "slaves" in retrospect in the school system. They were hardly treated as professionals, and society appeared to have never been concerned about their opinions and expressions.

I recall, after Mr. A shared that horrifying information with me, I was so disgusted until I had to take a couple of sick days, because I became totally depleted of energy. At that time, I would always worry about my students to whom I had been assigned, but I knew that I was unable to function under the mental condition that I was undergoing. After a couple of days being off, the time gave me the opportunity to re-group. I had flashbacks of all of the SexCessFully Promotions that I had witnessed. However, I concluded that regardless of what had happened, I was still going to maintain my morals, values and beliefs, and that I was not going to have sex to get a promotion. I continued to believe that someway, I would one day see justice serve in the school system.

CHAPTER SEVENTEEN

SOCIETY RECOGNITION

In spite of the injustice that I had witnessed during my tenure as a classroom teacher, I refused to have given up on the school system. I was determined that I was going to prove to the Commissioner that I would be able to get a promotion without having to engage in a sexual activity with any official from headquarters. Although, I was still feeling very angry, stressed, disgusted, and disappointed in the school system, I continued to attend relevant workshops and conferences. By attending these workshops and conferences, I no longer was focusing on qualifying myself for a promotion, but attended them to enhance my skills.

The more I became involved with the aforementioned, the more I had to explain to various individuals who were not in education why I had not received a promotion. Individuals in society would often times make comments in reference to my having obtained a variety of skills, and that I should have been assigned to a position that my skills and talents would have been best utilized to serve more students and teachers in the school system. Individuals in society would ask me, why didn't I apply for such positions. I dared to have shared with them that I had applied for many positions, and had been rejected, because I had refused to become sexually involved to secure such positions.

In my opinion, society seemed to have been naïve of the fact that SexCessFully Promotions were alive and doing well in our school system. In spite of all the television coverage that everyone had seen in reference to Justice Clarence Thomas and Ms. Hill. It appeared that individuals had just one mind set. Although, during the hearings between the two, people in society would comment on how some of them had been sexually harassed. In my opinion, I believe that for the reason of having been too afraid, the individuals who were experiencing sexual harassment during the same time of those two hearing felt that, because of lacking in popularity that it was no need in coming forward with such. Unfortunately, many times, individuals did not question how one had been chosen for positions. Even though some people had been promoted that did not have the skills, nor the tenure in the school system, but seemed to have been ignored as to why or how they qualified for such promotions.

During that time in my career, I began to wonder about the behavior of members in the society. It had always amazed me that no one talked about the possibility of sexual harassment or sexual involvement to receive a promotion. However, one in society did observe certain specific characteristics that certain people had in key positions. Some of the characteristics in females were that they were very shapely, and well groomed. Among the African Americans race, the females were of a lighter complexion, on the thinner size, and their hair was long, colored blonde or some light color. Among the Caucasian race, the females were thin, and would have long blonde free flowing hair. Very rarely did I observed females in top positions who were young, and who were overweight in reference to both races, as well as were very dark with short natural hair. However, there were overweight, very dark females in positions, but they were old, and had to work extremely hard to maintain their positions. It would always remind me of the "mammy" syndrome every time that I would see them in such position, because they appeared to have been the hardest workers among their colleagues. Nonetheless, these females appeared to have been among the top of the scale that really made the contributions to the school system that were needed.

After having observed these physical appearances among the females, I suspected even if I had not witnessed sexual engagement, I would have been somewhat curious as to why this type of pattern existed among the females in such key positions. It was not likely that females who had this type of image were the only ones in the school system that had talents, skills, and would have always met the criteria required to be selected for a top position.

I recall people from society imply to me that, because the way I looked, I should have been placed in a position that would have allowed me to be in the fore front. Each time someone would tell me this type of thing, I truly felt insulted, instead of complimented. I could not help but reflect back to the old cliché that females were just sex objects, and should be treated as such. Still, in our society, this type of thinking was going on. Also I would feel insulted and offended, because females appeared to have been willing to accept the fact that females would make good leaders, directors, superintendents, mayors and presidents. Nevertheless, this trend of thought appeared to have been the dominating factor that impacted upon as to what position a female would have received. This condition, in my opinion was just not relevant to education, but in every job market among professionals. Too often, females were like me. They were feeling very hopeless, and had to continue to suffer with the act of fear, underwent ongoing stress at all levels, all because of the way society had viewed and perceived them.

Fortunately, during this era, I was very much aware of how society had perceived females. Because of this awareness sometimes I would actually take on more activities than I really had the time. It was always that burning desire that I had within that I believed that things were going to get better, and that people would receive promotions based on their skills, talents, and experience. I believed that the image of beauty among society was going to change, and that, no longer all females would need to have the same type of characteristics, but a heterogeneous image would avail.

In addition, I recall communicating my perceived concepts in reference to the type of females who were in "key" positions to my colleagues. They would always respond by implying with a sensation of hopelessness and helplessness for that was the reason why they did not do anything. Because to try to improve their skills for advancement would have been a waste of their time and money, if there had been a cost involved. They also expressed the fact that they were convinced that sometimes they did not have the physical attractions (did not feel sexually appealing) to be interested in obtaining further skills that would have eventually lead to a promotion. They would mention often that they did not know the right people in charged.

Again, I was determined that I was not going to allow all of the pre-conceived concepts to prevent me from obtaining essential skills. Although, I knew that deep within, that my colleagues were telling the truth in reference to that it was really not about what one knew, how much experience one had, or the tenure, it was about who one knew, and what price one was willing to pay to obtain a position.

As time passed in education, some particular females appeared to have become more aware of how certain types of people kept receiving certain types of promotions. The greatest hardship that we had to undergo was that everyone was too afraid to share with members in society their observations. No one was willing to go forward with his/her perception of the most obvious. Females shared that they were afraid of losing their job, or having been labeled as a "trouble-maker," or perhaps, having to undergo unnecessary stress for having done so. Most females shared that it was easier for them to just keep silent. Moreover, they did discuss their feeling privately with other colleagues. They made sure that while sharing their feelings with other colleagues that no administrators were in proximity. In addition, one could not trust anyone. Very rarely, one trusted anyone who was not in the same position. For example, a teacher would trust another teacher, principal to principal, and on some occasions some people in the same positions did not trust each other. Determining factors for trust depended on how well one would observe his/her colleague, and that is, if He/she saw a teacher who was always grinning and conversing with the principal, the teachers on the same staff would always avoid sharing their inner feelings around that teacher.

Nonetheless, individuals in society who were, and were not educators continued to express to me their concerns in reference to why they thought that I should have been promoted, even after having won many awards, having done many televisions program, and radio talk shows. People in society continued having problems with trying to figure out that because of my diversified skills and talents that someone in authority must not have been aware of such, or perhaps they were not competent enough to have been in such position to make adequate decisions. Unfortunately, individuals in society were either not aware, or too afraid to have understood that a lot of positions were secured by SexCessFully Promotions. Therefore, in my opinion, when individuals in society recognize the aforementioned, they would serve as the messengers to alert others, particularly, if the messengers do not have a conflict of interest. That is, if the messengers are not employed by the same interest group. Although, I am aware that SexCessFully Promotions just do not occur in education, but from others who shared their stories who worked in other job markets. Again, it appears that, because of fear of having to lose a job, or position, it is my conviction that there will be no end to sexual harassment, and SexCessFully Promotions.

CHAPTER EIGHTEEN

THE EQUATION
(Stress Yields Depression)

Situations in the school system did not appear to have gotten any better as the years passed. As a matter of fact, they seemed to have gotten worst. I observed many of the younger females moved into key positions continuously. Some of these females had as little as five year tenure. However, they had all of the characteristics that many individuals had already perceived as the "key" to getting a promotion. These characteristics were that they were very shapely and sexually appealing. Moreover, because of the many promotions achieved in this manner, the decline in leadership, programs, support for students, teachers, principals, and implementation processes almost became null and void. However, the more seasoned classroom teacher had seen may programs that had been implemented, but were no longer in existence. The teachers had built up somewhat immunity to any concept that was mandated from the school system.

I recall, as the different programs would be identified and mandated for teachers to implement, teachers would immediately behave very negatively toward them. During this era, it was difficult to become optimistic about the programs, because all of us had been through the same process too many times. It was like following directions from the headquarters, not allowing oneself to become over enthusiastic, because we knew that sooner or later, they would have no long been in existence. Each time we were right about our perception.

On the other hand, I admit that some of the programs, if they had been maintained, and had competent people in charge of them would have made a vast difference, in reference to the improvement of students and teachers educational growth. Because of the lacking in expertise of the individuals who had been assigned to direct these programs, nothing of any value was effective. Too often, the SexCessFully Promotions were the individuals who had been chosen to direct these programs. Unfortunately, often times, they did not have the experience, skills or other relevant qualifications to have made these programs successful.

I recall after having read a bulletin that was posted at my school about a program, in my opinion, could have made an immediate positive impact on the growth of teachers and students performances in the entire school system. I knew that after many years of my having continued to acquire skills, and by having ongoing attendance at conferences and workshops, that I was more qualified for that position. Many of my colleagues approached me after having learned about the upcoming program, and suggested that I apply for the position, because they felt that under my leadership, the program would be very successful, and finally, a program that had the possibility to be ongoing. During this time, the teachers appeared to have tried to gain hope in the school system. I respected the comments and suggestions from my colleagues, thus I was motivated to apply for the position. Although, I had been through several rejections, because each time that I had applied for a position, it would seem that before the final decision was made, and because that I would not have sex with an executive, regardless of my skills, talents, and experience, I would always receive a rejection letter.

With the first experience of having been rejected, the memories had been instilled within me, or having witnessed various SexCessFully Promotions. I was not too eager to complete all of the required paper work for the position. Each time that I had applied for a position, I had been rejected, because I had refused to have sex. With great reluctant, I decided to follow the suggestions of my colleagues, and complete all the paper work required for the position. However, while doing the papers work for the position, I did not have to exert too much energy. I had been through this process too many times. It appeared that all criteria needed for completion of the paper work for all of the positions were synonymous. After having completed and forward the paper work to headquarters, I still did not have too much enthusiasm as in the past when I would submit applications. Anyway, I was very curious as to what type of feedback that I would have received. I thought that I had already experienced all of the types of rejections formats.

Meanwhile, I did not spend too much time concentrating on the outcome. I refused to have assumed that I would have been chosen for the position. I knew that every time in the past, just when I thought that I would have been chosen for a position, I was always wrong. Also I knew that after having met all criteria for the position, and that if the final decision factor would have been to have sex with an executive, I knew that another rejection letter would have been forthcoming. I was still determined that I was not going to have sex in order to receive a promotion, because I maintained my principles, morals and values.

Approximately, two weeks had passed, and in reality, I had forgotten that I had applied for the position. When I returned home from school, there was a letter from headquarters. This was the first communication that I had received since applying for the position. I opened and read the letter. The content simply was informing me that I had been scheduled for an interview on a particular date and time that did not excite me. I had been on interviews in the past, had scored very well, and what had mattered was still the "bottom line," and that was the ultimate deciding factor was a sexual activity with an executive from headquarters.

Nonetheless, when the date arrived for my interview, I adhered to all instructions that were indicated in the announcement that I had received. I would always arrive about 30 minutes early for an interview to relax, and allow time to collect my final thoughts. By now I knew the lay-out of the headquarters as well. I did not need specific directions from the receptionist upon entering the building. I went directly to the conference room that had been designated for the interview. Before I knocked on the door, I listened to try to figure out if there were people in the room.

I did not hear any voices or movement. I twisted the door knob and very quietly entered the empty room. There was a very small table and chairs with a lot of art work that had been placed haphazardly on the wall. The art work had been done by children from of the local elementary schools. This created the opportunity for me to utilize the time and not to have to sit at the table, appearing to have become idled when the executive arrived.

I was impressed with the quality of some of the art work. Some students were in grades as low as the second. I recall, standing in the hall, reading the names of the students and schools they attended, when a well- dressed gentleman passed. He did not speak, and went directly into the conference room. A few minutes later, two more individuals passed and went into the conference room. This time, it was a male and female. They left the door opened. From having listened briefly to their conversation, they knew each other very well. About five minutes before my scheduled interview, I entered into the conference room. I introduced myself, and asked them if I had come to the right place for the interview. They responded by saying, yes, and asked if I would take a seat. The seating arrangement had not been pre-arranged. I sat beside on gentleman, and the other two individuals were seated directly across from us. All the time, I was thinking that there must be others who were coming. The three showed no hurry to begin the interview.

After having talked with each other for a while, one of the gentlemen seemed to have taken the initiative to be the spokesperson, and leader for the group. However, I thought that it was somewhat rude, while the three of them talked and never included me into their conversation. I did not bother to create an opportunity to jump in, at will. The leader Mr. T (I will call him) started the interview dialogue by sharing with me that they had reviewed my documents, and all of the information included was very impressive, particularly with my diverse experience and achievement. Mr. T asked an opened-ended question which was, "why did I think that I should have been selected for that position, and if selected, what were my plans for implementations, evaluation, assessment, and monitoring?" Since I had practiced answering the same question several times, I had no problem answering the question, getting much better each time. I took my time, answered each question, but this time, I was able to support each statement with concrete documentation based on research that was current trends in education. I felt surprised with the way the answers flowed freely, without having to stumble or get lost and search for works. During the entire time of the interview, Mr. T was the only one who spoke. I recall observing the other two individuals who were sitting across the table form me, and concentrated on their expression. I noticed that the female appeared to have given the "thumbs-up" expression each that that I would speak. The male did not show too much reaction to anything. He appeared to not have been interested in what anyone said. For a moment, I began to wonder why the two had been invited.

When the interview was over, Mr T commended me for having done such an excellent job. He said that I was an excellent interviewer. These same compliments were confirmed by the other two. Mr. T implied that I was going to be selected for the position. Because of his positive attitude toward me, I began to feel, once again, enthusiasm, hope and excitement. I thought as I left that finally, I was going to receive a promotion without having to have sex. Once again, I was motivated, inclusively. I was able to perform much better at school. I became friendly to my family and colleagues, because my feeling was that at least, I could have proven to the Commission that I did not have to drop my draws as he had originally told me to receive a promotions.

A couple of days after the interview, I was paged on the PA system while at school to come to the main office, because I had a telephone call waiting. When I answered the call, it was Mr. T. Mr. T was very friendly, and asked if he could see me again back at the headquarters. No longer was I nervous, but very relaxed after having received Mr. T's request. My thinking was that during that re-scheduled meeting, Mr. T was going to assure me that I was going to be selected for the position, but he needed some more information for personnel. I gladly agreed to meet with him that was set for the next day.

I met with Mr. T in his office. The two of us were alone, that did not bother me. Mr. T had not shown any signs that he would have wanted to become sexually involved with me during the interview. Mt. T appeared that he followed the rules and regulations of the school system, and would not have taken any chances on doing anything that was not included in the regulations. While in Mr. T's office, he appeared to have been directing the reason for my having to come back to another type of thinking. During this visit, Mr. T asked me a lot of personal questions. Some of which were, if I were married, how many children did I have, and did I live alone. I was aware that this behavior was not relevant to the reason that I came back to his office. At first, I thought that he was demonstrating this type of behavior so I could relax. Unfortunately, when Mr. T found out that I lived alone, he asked if he could come and visit me at my house. That statement created an instant anger with me. I boldly told him no. After my reply, he talked two more minutes, and indicated for me to leave his office.

Shortly thereafter, I received a letter from headquarters. Once again, the content of this letter informed me that everyone was impressed with my credentials and achievements, but they regret having to tell me, that I was not selected for the position, and red further to wish me well in my career. In my opinion, this letter did not have a great impact on me immediately. As time passed, I began to eat more sweets, had problems sleeping, always felt angry, and often times would feel very sad for no apparent reason. It had become very difficult for me to function well in the classroom. It seemed that the students instantaneously became of a disciplinarian problem, and could hardly understand the subject matter. While at home, I did not feel like talking to my close friends and family. I was single, and refused to accept dinner invitations, or any other social invitations from the males whom I had been doing these kind of activities with for a long time. What I noticed, was that, no one said anything to me about the gradual change in my behavior. It was at this point, where I was buying new clothes, because the older clothes had gotten too small. The strange part about my behavior during this time was that I did not want to eat any vegetables, but only craved those food items that were complex carbohydrates. I was aware of the quick weight gain, and not to have cared.

The change came about as the results of one morning when my alarm sound, indicating the signal for getting up to go to school, and when

I attempted to get out of bed, I could not move. It was almost like an instant paralysis. I laid there for a while, and attempted again. This time I realized that I was suffering with a severe back problem. While still trying to force myself to take a bath, all of the vertebrae in my back seemed to have separated, and there was no movement. I was glad that I was near the telephone. I had become very frighten by now. I picked up the telephone and called one of my sisters who I knew was at home. I shared with her that I was having acute back pains. Immediately, she came to my house, helped me with my bath and dress, and took me to the hospital emergency room.

When the receptionist at the medical facility saw me upon entering, she called for medical assistance right away. I walked into to the emergency room, unable to sit or stand upright, and because of this appearance, this appeared to have frightened the receptionist. Two physicians came into the waiting area, and began to question me. They asked me to tell them what had happened to my back. They tried to help me stand upright, but the pain was too severe. A wheel chair was ordered at that moment, and they rolled me into the back to a private examination area. After having asked a series of basic questions, my reply to their questions was that I did not know what had happed to my back. They insisted that I had done some type of strenuous activity that was out of the ordinary to have caused such physiology. Meanwhile, they took X-rays, and administered a pain injection. They also performed various types of reflexes, etc. After a while, it was obvious that the pain medication had worked. I was able to finally sit and stand upright without having the severe pain. After the X-rays had developed, it was confirmed that my back's anatomy was fine, and that the X-rays did not show any obstruction. I was very pleased to have received that prognosis. Meanwhile, I was given a prescription for pain, and was told to stay home from work for a couple of days.

When I returned to work, I thought that everything was fine, until about mid-day. I experienced the same severe back symptom. I recall having to ask one of my colleagues to drive my car home for me. I was unable to sit upright, and close the door. Instead of my colleague driving me home, she drove me to my sister's house. (a registered nurse). When she saw me in such distress, she appeared to have been in a great deal of shock. Immediately, she dressed and took me directly to the hospital emergency room.

My private doctor was contacted by the attending physician in the emergency room to receive my medical records. The new staff reviewed very carefully the records, and looked very puzzled. They could not understand why there were no recordings that indicated some type of dorsal mal physiology. After having injected me with a pain killer, I was able to sit with a degree of comfort. The doctor began to ask the same questions in reference to the type of activities that could have been the contributors to such back pain. Again, I related the same information to them. I had not done any type of unusual activities, not even any type of exercise. I knew by now that I was truly undergoing severe stress attacks that had led to depression. I could not tell the doctor any details about the stressors, because I was too afraid of the consequences that would have been caused in the school system.

Nonetheless, the doctor informed me that I could not return to school until about three to four weeks. They put me on pain medication that would make a person very drowsy. Therefore, it would have been unsafe for me to work with children. I noticed that while away from the school, I did not experience any severe back pains. While I was at home recovering, I thought that the doctor would have told me that they needed to discuss my case further, so that they would be able to treat my condition more adequately. During this era, "manic depression" had not become a household expression, and that many medical individuals had not identified it as such. However, the doctor concluded that there were some other type of stimuli that were causing my problem, because they were not able to identify the causative agent of my problems.

After having returned to the doctors after three weeks of having been away from the school system, the doctors could not reach an agreement between them that I should continue to work for the duration of that school year. Therefore, they wrote letters to the necessary authorities, and informed that that because of my condition, I would no longer be able to perform the duties that were required for a classroom teacher.

This news, in the beginning appeared to have added even more stress. I recall the principal calling my house, two and three times per week, asking when would I be able to return to school. Those telephone calls irritated me, because it appeared that the principal incenuated that I was deliberately being negligence, although, he had received the communication from my doctors that clearly stated that it was imperative that I stayed away from the school system the duration of the school year. It had become very difficult and annoying to stay home every day. I had always been very active since I could remember. As the boardomness continued, I had no other choice but to contact my doctors, and express such. My doctors suggested that it might be helpful, if I would change my environment for a while. He suggested that if financially possible, take a trip to an island, etc.

The timing seemed to have been perfect. I had been invited to visit Singapore with all expense paid. I shared with my doctor, and he told me that an Island like Singapore would have been the perfect place for me to go. I could have imagined that the doctor knew, once in Singapore, the culture and physical environment would have been so different, until there would not have been anytime to concentrate on the school system.

I waited about two weeks before I took the trip to Singapore. I must admit that upon arriving in Singapore that was a total cultural shock. I could not have concentrated on the school system if I had tried. My total effort while in Singapore was trying to adapt to the environment was very tropical. It was very hot and humid. The month was February. The geographic was beautiful. There were gigantic tropical plants that blossomed in different colors all along the freeways. The country appeared to not have had people living there, because of its cleanliness, and no crime. The natives and other expiates were extremely friendly, kind and very courteous. I never heard profanity while on the streets, and did not see any type of trash on the street, not even a cigarette butt.

I recall appreciating what I had seen. I had come from just the opposite. As time passed, I began to receive invitations to visit with their educational systems. Someone had informed the various ministries that I was an American, and had a science and education background. The Singaporeans were very impressed with America's Educational System. Unlike, what I had experienced in America. They respected skills and talents, and did not have problems with making it known. Shortly, I received a call from the National University of Singapore. The caller had received word that I was in the country, and asked if I would be willing to come to the university and speak with the students and staff. I felt very elated, because I had not expected to have been invited that quickly to share anything with anyone. However, I accepted the invitation without reservation. I did not know what to expect from the university, because he did not give me any specific topic. The caller said that, the university was anxiously awaiting for my visit. I was not intimidated by the invitation, because I had read a lot about their educational system, as well as had talked with some of the natives, and had acquired more information. That was why I felt very comfortable meeting with them.

Back in America, I continued learning about the current trends in education, particularly, in science. In addition, I had already gained information and knowledge from the natives. The day of the meeting, one of the officials from the university picked me up from my residence. During the drive to the university, I learned a great deal more that helped me to envision as to how I would have started my dialogue, once having met with the students and staff.

The time for my presentation, the spokesperson introduced me by exemplifying overwhelming enthusiasm, and appreciation of the fact that I had accepted the invitation to share with them. The introduction set the stage so well, until for the first time, I began to recognize that there were people who could appreciate one's talent. I shared with the audience, an overview of my experience and background in Science Education. At the conclusion of my presentation, I allowed the audience to ask any kind of questions about education. They asked very interesting and intellectual questions. In addition, the staff and students extended high compliments in reference to my presentation. The individual who had invited me informed me that he was going to be sharing with the President of the university the impact that I had made with the staff and students. This was the first time during my tenure in education that I truly felt appreciated and respected for my skills.

Shortly after had spoken at the university of Singapore, I received a letter from the Dean of the university. The content of the letter was to inform me of a position at the university. They offered me an Assistant Professorship in the School of Medicine. I could not believe what I was reading at that moment. The letter continued to explain that the only documentation needed was a copy of my degrees, passport and birth certificate.

Since I had witnessed a great deal of SexCessFully Promotions within the schools system back in America, immediately, I was entertaining the thought of what price would I have to pay if I had accepted the position. While still a bit curious, I returned to the university to meet with the top authorities to confirm that the position offered was legitimate as well as to test for any sexual seducers that could have been waiting for the price, so to speak. During our conversation, everyone was very polite and professional. There was absolutely no indication of sexual harassment. However, they, collectively, shared that they wanted me to take the position that had been offered. Somehow, I kept waiting for a telephone call that would have informed me that I had to meet with one of the university's officials privately, and, in my opinion, that would have given rise to a sexual activity. To my surprise, this never happened. The only thing happened during the telephone calls, was that they tried to convince me why I should take the post. In some instances, they offered to increase the starting salary.

Finally, I wrote a letter to the Dean and thanked him for the offer. I informed him that I had to return to my school system in America. I did not know that the Dean had written a letter to the Mayor of my City, and the Superintendent of the School System informing them how privileged and appreciative that they had been by having one their outstanding teachers to hare with them some educational concepts and principles. The letter continued to congratulate both of them for having such a dedicated, talented and skilled teacher in their system. A copy of the letter was sent to me.

A week later, I received a letter from the Dean of Academics from the University of Indonesia, at Jakarta. This letter was inviting me to come to their university to share the same type of information that I had shared in Singapore with their students and staff. This was an all paid trip. I did not hesitate to agree to share with the university educational trends, as well as my experience as a Science Educator. My speaking in Indonesia, in my opinion, was more profound than while in Singapore. By now, I felt very confident, because of the individuals feedback, while at the National University of Singapore. I followed the same format, while in Indonesia, as I had in Singapore.

After the conclusion of my presentation, I allowed time for feedback, comments, and questions. Once again, the participants demonstrated that they were most impressed, and had been introduced to may concepts and principles that were applicable to the university's academia. The official from the university, like from Singapore sent a letter to my city officials, expressing the same as Singapore.

Meanwhile, back in Singapore, I recall experiencing more compliments, and have made presentations at privately owned schools, and some of the local schools. By this time in my life, I no longer had any symptoms of back problems, or any type of depression. Once I believed in a system. It was most appreciated to have witnessed individuals in key positions, who had the ability to recognize qualifications in others, and knew how to best utilize their talents.

During my entire stay in Singapore, I never witnessed, or even heard of any type of discussion in reference to one having received a SexCessFully Promotion. This was evident by the way their educational system progressed. I compared the difference between their school system's operation and progress with the same of our school system back in America. The most obvious difference between the two was that in Singapore, individuals were appointed to positions who had met the essential criteria and qualifications for such. The school system in which I worked in America, many of the individuals appointments were based on sexual engagement, friends, members of sororities, fraternities, churches, and other social clubs, in other words, it was who one knew, and to what organizations one belonged.

Another observation that I made, while analyzing the Singapore Educational System, was that in reference to females, it did not matter about the physical appearance, or ethnic background. I saw a diversified group of individuals in positions. In addition, to help with the confirmation of my comparison, I would, on various occasions, ask the type of questions that would provide the answers that I was seeking for this confirmation. I recall asking one female executive about SexCessFully Promotions. Her response was that someone would have told, and the individuals who were victims of such, both males and females would have been dismissed from the school system immediately.

After she shared her most genuine answer to that question with me, all I could think about was how could one in America inform the necessary authorities, who did not have a conflict of interest in the school system of all the SexCessFully Promotions that I had witnessed. I was also convinced, because SexCessFully Promotions were part of the down fall of our school system. The school system had continued to regress during my tenure. In my opinion, the regression in the school system was the result of so many unqualified individuals in key positions. In addition, to our school system's problem was that once in a position, the individuals stayed. It appeared to have never been a concern or mattered about the negative reports, the standardized test scores getting lower each year, and more money was allocated to Special Education, instead of hiring more teachers to reduce class size. It seemed that the total management in the school was completely out of existence. Although, many programs had been introduced and implemented, they did not last very long, because of the incompetence of the individuals who were in charge. Therefore, it was my Prayer to someday come forward, and share my comparison and conviction.

After several months passed, nearing the end of August, I began to think about the upcoming school year back in America. Although, I had been offered very appealing positions in Singapore, I was more convinced that I had to come back to America, and seriously use my God's given talent to help the students in our school system. I had almost forgotten about the SexCessFully Promotions, and had tried very hard to put my past behind.

A couple of days before I knew that schools were going to open for the next school year, I telephoned the principal of the school of which I had been assigned. He was very pleased to have heard from me. During our conversation, I asked if my position had been filled, his response was no. Without hesitation, I told him that as soon as I contacted my travel agent, I would be back to teach again. I remember the happiness that the principal exemplified during the telephone call. I also appreciated his support and willingness to share with me how much had had appreciated my effort, and the willingness to return. I sent a letter to all of the Institutions in Singapore, that were so desperately wanting me to be a part of their system. I thanked all of them, but informed them that I was returning to America. I was convinced that it was in America's School System where my skills and talent were needed.

CHAPTER NINETEEN

BACK IN AMERICA

(Return to the School System)

School for teachers had already begun when I returned to America. When I arrived to my assigned school, everyone greeted me with such love, until it appeared that I was experiencing a metamorphosis. As the day passed, the principal received a call from headquarters, informing him that I had not been released from being under doctor's care. Although my name had not been removed from the staffing at my school, headquarters had received the notification from the attending physician that informed them of the reason why I could not perform my regular duties as a classroom teacher. Therefore, I was instructed by headquarters to see their physician so that if at all possible, they would have made the final decision for me to return to work.

I recall leaving the school to adhere to those instructions. When I arrived at the school system's health department, a physician had been assigned to my case, and not waste any time in seeing me. The technique that he used for final prognosis was so incidental, until I concluded that I definitely would not have gone to him had I had serious health problems. He never performed any tests. The only thing that he did during this visit was to review my previous medical record that was forward from my private doctor, and asked a few questions. After which, he asked if I thought that I could return to work, and perform the duties of a classroom teach. However, he did share other options. The other options were to either terminate all of my duties as a classroom teacher, and or go into administration, or to terminate all duties of an educator, and go on total disability. At that time, and because of having experienced such positive feedback while in Asia, I felt so great, and once again, had regained confident in education. I was determined not to have gone out on disability. Even though, I suspected that the problems that were the contributors to the severe stress that had led to my depression initially, may have still been in existence in the school system. I elected to return to the classroom, and asked the physician to write a release form. The physician appeared to have been very reluctant to writing the release form. However, he did include certain specific instructions in the form.

It was the first day of school for the students. My scheduled included three different science preparations and five classes. Each class was the size of three classes in one. As I looked at the students upon entrance, I would weep silently for them. I knew that my task was going to be very difficult during that school year, even if I had not been instructed to limit my activities, because there were just too many students assigned to one person. It was no need in informing the principal of this major problem, because most teachers were experiencing the same type of problem. When a teacher would inform the principal, he/she would make it very clear that there was nothing could be done, even if he/she asked for more staff. It was very obvious that the decision-makers from the school system's headquarters were not interested in the students' progress and achievement. During that era, it appeared that the focus was on maintaining discipline. Therefore, if a teacher could have done that, nothing else seemed to have mattered.

The observation, in all reality was ongoing throughout the school system. Society continued to question the decline in test scores, and the graduates lacking in basic skills. Moreover, for teachers, most of us knew that graduated did not have the basic skills. In some cases, the graduates hardly knew how to follow basic directions to complete a standard form application for employment. In addition, I recall reading the statistics in reference to the number of high school graduates who entered post-secondary institutions, compared to the number of high school graduates who actually finished. The conclusion was that in comparing the statistics by race, both whites and blacks, 87% of black students compared to 83% of whites students did not finish a degree program.

Although, this information was very alarming, that did not surprise me. As a classroom teacher, and having been assigned to super large classes, I knew that by working with the students daily, did not have the essential skills. Unfortunately, because of some individuals who had been placed in key positions, that would have afforded them the opportunity to have monitored this adverse condition were not competent, because many of them had been SexCessFully Promoted.

Nonetheless, the school year was passing very quickly. I felt like a beginning teacher. I had been relieved from the major stress symptoms that I had undergone prior to my break. My energy level was very high, and I was very eager to take on more creative and innovative concepts and principles with my students. I became so involved with my students, until I forgot about the restrictions that the physician had instructed for me. I was back to my old habits again. I did not sit, in other words, I became even more involved and physically active with the students. As mentioned, I was no longer mentally entertaining the antagonizing negative forces that had previously dominated my motivation. I was able to maintain my aggressive behavior in the classroom for three months into the school year before I had a minor setback. I recall very distinctly, after having assigned the students a lab that involved working with microscopes, once again, my back seemed to have just snapped temporarily. I could always track down the causative agent in reference to the problem. Because of major inadequate supplies, materials, equipment, and overcrowded classes, there were four students assigned to one microscope.

After having demonstrated as well as having allowed individual students to practice using them before the lab time, the students showed evident of still having not mastered the skills of having learned how to properly use the microscope. Therefore, while in the lab, because of the students deficiency in skills, they were calling me to assist them continuously. Without having the time to concentrate on my ailment, I would respond to each of them lending my help. I recall that when a group of students asked me to come to their station, I rushed to assist them, and when I slightly bent to look to adjust their microscope, I knew something strange had happened to my back. Before I attempted to straighten back up, I said a little prayer. I was not too sure if I were going to be able to stand erect or not. All I could think about was trying not to alarm all of my students. While trying to ease back up, I pretended that I needed more time to find the specimen, and stayed in the bent position, because at that moment, I was in so much pain.

Meanwhile, I was too afraid to call my doctor, because of the fear of having to take another leave of absence. I could not trust having to go on leave again, because I suspected that I would have been advised to go on disability. As I thought about the other options, that the school system's physician had shared, and that was to have been given and administrative position, I was too convinced already, that eventually, I would have been placed into a situation with an executive who would have perhaps warranted a sexual affair. I did not want to go through any of that sexual harassment anymore.

Moreover, during the remaining of the school year, and because of my observations of the students in Singapore, it was much easier for me to come up with more creative and innovative methods of teaching. Although in Singapore, the class sizes were very small. Each school was identified by different colors of uniforms. A student dared not to have been properly dressed upon the arrival of school. The teachers in the schools did not have to undergo disciplinarian problems, unlike in some American schools. In my school system, often times discipline was the dominating factor in a classroom. Many times, teachers have very little support from the school based administrators, and because of the lacking in support, many teachers are stressed out, and continue to feel hopeless, as well as helpless.

During my teaching tenure, I have known administrators who really wanted to support teachers. Unfortunately, they were too afraid of the individuals in key positions from the headquarters. I recall that in spite of the cover-up of all kind of problems in the school system, some administrators took a stand, and attempted to correct problems in their assigned school. Usually, when they took on this type of authority, the administrator was transferred, or would have eventually leave the school system, because of failing to adhere to the reprimand from the higher authorities. In addition, during my early years of teaching, I was assigned to a junior High school, and witnessed a student attack a teacher. The principal asked headquarters to transfer the student to another school and was declined. The principal told the authorities at headquarters that either the student be removed, or he would quit. The authorities in essence, implied that the principal was trying to be a "trouble-maker" in the school system, and proceeded to try to reprimand the principal. Finally, with no support, the principal quit, and did not return to the school system.

Nevertheless, I knew that I could not have made a vast difference in trying to relate my experience to the top authorities in the school system, because I knew that many of the positions had been obtained by SexCessFully Promotions. In my opinion, when one is SexCessFully Promoted, one takes on the "puppet" syndrome. That is, one is always controlled by that individual who holds the "torch," so to speak over the person's head.

Although, with my having to deal with all of the aforementioned adversities, I continued to try to improve the educational growth for the students to whom I had been assigned. However, it was very difficult trying to overcome all of the "red" tape. I would still exert a great deal of energy to provide my students with high quality skills, as well as continued to have high expectation of them. Every opportunity that I would get, I would make arrangement for them to take field trips, etc. This was very difficult, because I could not take all of my students. Therefore, I would allow the students who had not been severe disciplinarian problems to go on the trips.

My attitude had changed since my brief stay in Singapore. Therefore, during the remaining of the school year, I recall having to experience some unpleasant behavior form the local and top authorities. They appeared to have not been able to perceive the needs of the students. By the end of the school year, I experienced my motivation gradually becoming depleted, due to the lacking of support and perhaps, having to continue to try and relate to incompetent individuals in top positions, who in my opinion, often times had been SexCessFully Promted.

CHAPTER TWENTY

THE WINNING OF AWARDS

(Refused to Give Up)

In spite of feeling very helpless and hopeless, I was still determined to help to make a change in the school system. At the close of the school year, instead of traveling that summer as usual in the past, I decided that I would seek the opportunity to create some type of networking. My focus was not on the authorities at headquarters, or elected officials. My thinking was geared toward seeking support from non-titled individuals in other institutions. Therefore, I was fortunate enough to have met a gentleman who was working at NIH (National Institute of Health). During our conversation, he was able to detect my frustration with the school system. He informed me that I could contact Ms. P (I will call her) at NIH. Ms. P was the top officer, who was instrumental in assisting individuals with new concepts and principles. I telephoned her, and during the conversation Mr. P was very receptive to what I shared with her. She arranged for the two of us to meet to discuss further options. The meeting was scheduled on the campus of NIH. It was scheduled at the end of June. Before this meeting, I had never been on the campus of NIH, but had seen the sign many times. I had figured out how long it would have taken me to arrive by automobile. Upon arrival, Ms. P met me in the lobby, and escorted me to her office. She was in her mid-thirties, very thin, free flowing blonde hair, and very well dressed. I experienced a quick flashback that was recalling the characteristics of the individuals who would have been, more than likely, SexCessFully Promoted to have obtained such position. This thought was momentarily. Ms. P was very friendly, and appeared to have been pleased with my appearance.

During our dialogue, she shared with me that the Johns Hopkins School of Nursing was looking for someone with my credentials and experience for a summer internship. She asked if I were interested in giving it a try. I really did not expect that, but my answer was yes. While I sat in her office, she telephoned the Dean of Nursing at Johns Hopkins School of Nursing, and shared with her, (Ms. M I will call her) that she had someone in her office that was willing to fill that post. Again, more surprises, because Ms. P had not asked too much about my educational background, but was impressed with my having shared a variety of experiences. Moreover, Ms. M asked to speak with me. During our conversation, arrangement was made for me to come to the School to complete all paper work, and tour the facility.

As I prepared to leave Ms. P's office, she kept thanking me for having contacted her. She shared that she would like to see me on other occasions that were not work related. She invited me to come and spend the weekend with her at her home. She told me that she had purchased a large house, lived alone, and was not married. When Ms. P first started talking, I thought that she was just being polite and hospitable. I had no "clue" that Ms. P was inferring that I had to pay the price for her assistance with me getting on board at Johns Hopkins School of Nursing. Ms. P walked with me to my car, still insisting that I came back to spend time with her over the weekend. I was flawed. I really did not know what to say. In my opinion, Ms. P appeared to have been a lesbian by evidence of her conversation. However, I was very careful with not having to offend her. I told her that I would contact her before the weekend. I knew that was going to be the last time that I had planned to have been in Ms. P's presence alone. I left, never called Ms. P as promised, and she never contacted me.

The time had come for me to meet with Ms. M. I was a little paranoid by now. However, upon arriving to Ms. M's office, I was a photograph of her family. This was a sign that she was married, with children. Knowing this information up front helped to make me feel very comfortable, and that I did not have to entertain split thought processes during the meeting. She exemplified great enthusiasm and appreciation throughout the meeting. She shared with me why and how the School of Nursing could benefit from my expertise, as well as informed me that a greater possibility existed to extend the networking further. Next, we toured the facility. While walking through the hallways, I observed blown up pictures of post Deans, and individuals who had graduated from the school. I became alarmed with what I saw. I mentioned to Ms. M that I was pleased with what I had seen, because there were no African-Americans, Hispanics, Indians or Asians in any of the pictures. She concurred with me that she too, was alarmed with the concept of not having other ethnic groups involved. She made it clear to me that is why she needed for me to have accepted the position.

My duties during this internship were very minimal. I did a research project that did not require too much of my time, and lectured to Human Anatomy and Physiology to the potential graduates. Meanwhile, Ms. M contacted the School of Medicine Research Department, and informed one of the researchers who had just received a million Dollars Grant that I was on board, and asked if she would take a day or so to share with me some of the research that she was doing. The arrangement was made and confirmed between the two that I could spend one week in her department. While spending one week with Dr. B (I will call her) and opportunity became available so that I could meet other researchers in various capacities of medicine. Each of the researchers, like Dr. B had also received million dollars grants. My present teaching assignment in the school system was teaching Anatomy and Physiology and Microbiology. During my stay at the School of Medicine Research, I met "key" individuals who were doing research in the subdivisions that I taught in Microbiology. Therefore, I knew the subject matter very well, but never had adequate materials and supplies from the school system to apply such in the classroom.

The staff was very impressed with my knowledge, and offered assistance for me when I returned to my classroom. They provided lots of updated materials and supplies. In addition, we established a partnership, whereas my students had the opportunity to do internship at the hospital. After having completed my internship at Johns Hopkins, schools opened. I was assigned to teach the same courses, but with a greater deal of knowledge, and a direct network system with Johns Hopkins. It wasn't until Johns Hopkins highlighted me in that monthly newspaper, the school system finally recognized my skills and talent. It was because of this experience, my school began to focus on the Allied Health Careers, including classes in EMT, Physical Therapy, Nursing, Medical Technology 1 and 2, and established a Dental Lab. These programs were getting attention in many states by now. The school system recognized that my involvement with Johns Hopkins was really getting position attention, especially when the authorities at headquarters read and saw in the media that NBC News had come down and shadowed me all day, beginning at my school, and ending at Johns Hopkins. At his point in my career, I no longer had fear, and or was thinking about sexual harassment and rejection from the school system.

Time passed, and while at home, I received a call from Ms. C (I will call her) who shared with me that I had been selected to complete the process for "teacher of the year" for the school system. Each district had to choose one teacher to represent. There were 8 people (elementary, middle and senior high school) who had been selected from my school system. Each of us had to complete 12 essay questions for the selection process. After the submission of the questions, each was scheduled for an interview. There were 15 people from diverse background served on the interview panel. During the interview, each asked two questions with follow up comments. The questions were geared toward experience and academics. I observed from the expressions and covert feedback that I had done a satisfactory job.

A week later, Ms. C called, and informed me that I had been selected as the best high school teacher, and pausing for a moment, said that I had been selected as the best school system teacher out of a total of over 800 hundred. She congratulated me, and asked how did I feel. I felt great, because I really did not expect to hear that good news. During the fall, the state and each school district attended a live televised broadcast, hosted by local television personalities. At the broadcast, each of us received many outstanding awards, and the state map with our name on it presented by the governor. I was also given the Mayor's Educational Fund for Excellence award that included $2000.00 and an IBM Think Pad laptop. I continue to make many television appearances, and host many educators from several states.

As this news spread, I received a call from the Afro-American Newspaper, stating that I had been nominated by a pastor, and was among of the 12 finalists requested to appear at a local university for the selection of "Woman of the Year" award for my city. The award was given by the Afro-American Newspaper and the Greyhound Bus Company. I was told that I could have invited unlimited guests, while others were limited to five. The time for the ceremony had come, and there were speakers, pictures were taken for the newspaper, etc. Finally, everyone was congratulated and thanked for having contributed to society, and asked to return to our seats. One member from the judges began to read the third placed winner, it was not me, then the second place winner, again not me. When he began to read what the first place winner had contributed, everything he said was what I had done. It really didn't appeal to me that they were getting ready to call my name for woman of the year, until he did. This was a great moment in my life.

When I returned from spending another summer in Singapore, I had received many messages to contact an owner of Kentucky Fried Chicken, and McDonald Enterprise. After having contact both, each informed me that I was the recipient of their award, which again was televised. In addition, the state general assembly legislative branch, both house and senate collectively gave me 45 awards that same time period. Thereafter, I was invited to serve on many boards from the city to the state, and most of which I was the chairperson, and or president. I was no longer entertaining fear, stress and depression having to worry about when and how would I be recognized from the school district, and needless to mention no more rejection letters, etc. because I refused to have become SexCessFully Promoted.

CHAPTER TWENTY-ONE

AN ABRUPT CHANGE IN ADMINISTRATION

(A Recapitulation of the Same Ole Soup)

During this era, an election year was forthcoming. The elected official who wanted to be re-elected had to come up with a serious platform to attract the constituents' votes. They began to actively focus on all the publicized negativism in reference to the local school system. They began to introduce words such as, accountability, information, inclusion, etc. Never did anyone mention the words such as fairness, sexual harassment, and or SexCessFully Promotions.

The incumbent elected officials began to find major fault in the current school system's operation, including top executives, as well as the teaching staff. Very briefly, without having placed too much emphasis, they mentioned parental involvement and responsibility for their children. It was always very painful to have witnessed individuals who were competent being left out of the decision-making process that would have improved and impacted upon the school system. The individuals who were omitted were always the teachers and school based administrators. As a teacher, it bewildered me, as I would read about the school system hiring an outsider, creating the title of a consultant. Often times, it was an individual who had been dismissed, because of poor performance in another capacity. The consultant role was to be the brain behind what we, as the teachers and school based personnel needed to have improved the education of the children in the school system. Many of these individuals were hired, and many times, from my observation, teachers were omitted. Therefore, the rationale behind such behavior has never been clear to me, and other school-based personnel.

It appeared that if one had been very serious about making a change, one should have gathered data from reliable sources that could have adequately helped with the solutions to the problems that existed. As mentioned prior, the news media were excellent at reporting the negative things that were going on the system, but rated unsatisfactory in high-lighting individuals who were achievers, including students, teachers and administrators. Meanwhile, since teachers had continued to have been omitted from the "healing" process, so to speak, it appeared that teachers had very little enthusiasm or confidence in the methods and techniques that the higher epsilon used. As a classroom teacher, I would always conclude, that the current process that was used was just a recapitulation of the same ole soup. Arriving at this conclusion was simple, because the key players who were the school based personnel were usually omitted from the decision-making planning process. However, on few occasions, I do remember having read about a teacher or two input. Although, this happened, there would never be any change in reference to the existing problems in the school system. Very often, I would wonder to what criteria had been used to select the particular teacher, and I would always ask myself the same question, which was, "which one of the component in the selection criteria was used to identify the teachers, was it the one component that included/focused on SexCessFully Promoted?"

Nonetheless, another election year had arrived, and the politicians were working very hard on their campaign trail. All of whom continued to promise, if elected, what they were going to do to help the troubling school system. All of the promises that we heard, and had read about sound terrific, but we had heard all of this type of political jargon before, and had not witnessed any progress. However, we had witnessed continuous regression in the school system. Therefore, it appeared that teachers and other school based personnel had very little hope and faith as to what the politicians were promising while campaigning.

It was very hard to have convinced those of us who were in the schools that the politicians were serious about what they were say, because we could not recall having seen anyone visiting the schools to which we had been assigned. Needless to mention, conversing with a school based employee, or the students as to how they would be able to help with their needs. During this time in education, most of the incumbents were re-elected. Many of them did not need time to become familiar with the trends in politics. They continued business as usual. I recall the issue, in reference to the problems in the school system had to be addressed immediately. Therefore, the focus was on such. Society and educators alike, began to have high hope, while anticipating an immediate change in the school system.

The elected officials and the mayor of the city concluded that the change had to start at the top. They proceeded to work on making the change. At the end of the school year, communications were that by the conclusion of the school year, a new change at the top was forthcoming for the upcoming school year. This was a welcoming promise. I recall anxiously awaiting for this change to occur. Although, deep within, I did not believe that a dramatic change would have been forthcoming, regardless of the change in personnel at headquarters, because one of the main reason for such deficiency and regression in the school system was the result of SexCessFully Promotions. Unfortunately, no one was talking about this very important behavior between individuals who were involved. I believed that an abrupt change in the operation within the school system would not happen. I had seen too many changes in the school system, and the result had always been new faces, but a recapitulation of the same ole soup.

Shortly, before the end of the school year, a change in the top executives at headquarters had taken place. It was not good business strategy to clean house, so to speak, because it is practical to retain some of the individuals who had the expertise to assist the incoming team. Unfortunately, it appeared that some of the individuals who were retained were not the most competent, because in some instances, they had been SexCessFully Promoted, and did not have the acquired essential skills and qualification to have made a change in education. Without having individuals who were in decision-making positions, and having done further investigation, would have been just a recapitulation of the same ole soup, and therefore, would have been no progress.

The new executives were in placed at the headquarters before the end of the school year. Usually, at the end of a school year, teachers were so exhausted, until there would be little concentration on what was happening at headquarters. My focus was on taking that most necessary break of getting out of school so that I could get rid of another year's built up stress. During the summer months, there was not too much mentioned in reference to any changes that were being made under the new leadership.

The opening of schools for the new school year was approaching. The teachers had about one more week of vacation. I recall after having returned to my city, I did not bother to ask anyone what was happening with education, because as mentioned throughout this dialogue, I had very little faith in the integrity of the school system. Nevertheless, I remember the first day for staff at the opening of school, all the teachers who had been assigned to my school were in place for a faculty meeting. While waiting for the principal to arrive, the secretary came into the meeting, and informed us that the principal had called, and was going to be about 40 minutes late. We were instructed not to leave the room. Meanwhile, a gentleman who was on the staff decided to imitate the higher executives. He went to the chalk board, and began to list several made-up acronyms. All of which would have been a continuation of degrading classroom teachers. Most of the teachers laughed, while they gave input and made up more acronyms for the gentleman to list on the board. I did not think that the list of acronyms was very comical. I had a very serious attitude toward the students, as well as my conviction that a change could happen, and therefore I refused to succumb to the jokes. It appeared that during the past, everything that had been tried in the school system ended up being a joke. That is why everyone in that faculty meeting could relate to what the gentleman was doing.

The principal arrived approximately one hour later. The day of school has always virtually been the same since my tenure in education. Each school term, teachers would be told that changes had been made, and that the old traditional habits would no longer be tolerated. However, as time passed during the year, no one appeared to have been adhering to any of the initial directions. After a couple of months passed, everything would always be back to normal. It appeared not to have matter about evaluations. There were no incentives for teachers in the school system to which I had been assigned. Therefore, teachers who always worked very hard, helped raised students test scores, and other academic essentials, always continued to do the same. It did not matter whether a teacher was rated excellent, and or unsatisfactory treatment toward both was the same. Regardless, there were no raise, no rewards, and no kind of signs of appreciation bestowed upon them. However, in many cases, I could have seen SexCessFully Promotions, if I would have adhered to the Commissioner's comments and directions that he had shared with me during the beginning of my teaching career.

During the meeting, the principal shared with the staff the expectations that had been passed on from headquarters. As we viewed the mandates from headquarters, there were no significant difference changes made, except for the introduction of a couple of new words that once again, were directed for the teachers only. The new words were accountability, efficacy, and Performance goals. It was amazing that individuals at headquarters thought that these words were some "new" in education. It did not take very long after having received the mandate that the so-called new vocabulary strategy was just a recapitulation of the same ole soup.

Already, I was disturbed and displeased about the qualifications of the new experts who had been selected in top positions at headquarters. This disturbance and displeasure were the result of having read the current mandate. My conclusion was that, if one were not aware that teachers were already, or should have been efficient in their discipline, and needless to mention that when the teachers were hired, it should have been evident that the teachers had met the criteria for the job. Therefore, reformation were to be successful, the individuals in the decision-making positions should have recognized and started with correcting the cause of the failures that included, the over crowed classes, the lacking of adequate supplies, materials and equipment, and the hiring of incompetent individuals to direct special programs.

Unfortunately, in spite of the aforementioned, teachers were still being battered with the new vocabulary. It was my conviction, that teachers did not have any problem with the new vocabulary. The problem was with the decision-makers who had omitted the most important ingredients for the completion of the mandate. It continued to cause pain with me when teachers continued to be omitted from the decision-making processes that affected their students. A major solution could have been to hire more classroom teachers to reduce class size, and allocate more funds to the individual schools to be able to purchase the essentials for a smooth operation of the schools.

Nonetheless, under the abrupt change in administration, we continued to observe the hiring of more executives, instead of classroom teachers. The class sizes became larger, etc. It appeared to have been a major communication gap between the local school and headquarters. I recall from time to time, visiting headquarters because frustration, I was bold enough to talk to key people in decision-making positions. This created more frustration while trying to relate to such individuals, because they appeared to have been not in touch with reality. I would talk with females at the headquarters. They appeared to have been listening more. Most of the time, the feedback from both agenda would always be that no one appeared to have been collectively, making-decisions that would have benefited students in the school system. Sadly, I did not witness too much accountability in reference as to why some of the positions were needed.

Finally, the year passed, and under the newly appointed administration, again, there was absolutely no change at the local schools. As a matter of fact, things were getting worst, in comparison with previous years. I did notice, however that at headquarters, I saw more youthful looking well-dressed individuals. Therefore, from years of observation, good and bad in the school system, my thought was that, could this change to much younger executives be the result of more SexCessFully Promotions.

CHAPTER TWENTY-TWO

THE INTERVIEW

Part One

(Tried to Keep Hope Alive)

It was nearing the close of the school year when we as teachers became aware that they system was going to make a drastic change in leadership. This change was needed according to sources, because of the continuous attendance problems, low test scores, and they system continuing to rate lower that its counterpart. Another school year had passed. Educators were anxiously awaiting with enthusiasm and curiosity, and as always wishing for the best for the students. Once again, anxiety appeared to have been surfacing after many disappointments with the existed administration. As the new administrations was selected, appointed and confirmed by our local government, staff members were excited and hoping to see a difference in the system that not only would have improved the students image, but also the school-based staff, particularly morale.

The new administration was finally in place. We, the staff continued to observe the type of communication that appeared to have collaboratively began to build upon what was already in place, as well as attempted to be a little more innovative and creative, focusing on fresh ideas in hope to delete the negative publicity of the existing system. As time passed, and after having reviewed the communications (the few that teachers received), my morale and enthusiasm became very "pumped", so to speak. Again, I was hoping that maybe this is the administration that will finally recognize the system's talents, and would be able to identify those individuals with the qualifications, skills, experience, and or expertise, that they would choose such individuals based on such for a key position that would help to bring the system up to standards. I was seriously hoping that the time was finally here, or would have been forthcoming, and that SexCessFully Promotions would have been coming to an end.

Unfortunately, this thinking was very far from the truth. It all started with a telephone call from a gentleman, Mr. T (I will call him) who was not affiliated with education. During our brief conversation, he asked if I knew Mr. Y, I said no. Mr. T said that I should get to know him, and that I should give him a call and set up a meeting with him. Mr. T knew that I was well diversified, had done extensive travel, and had won many awards for excellence in education. Mr. T tried to convince that Mr. Y would bring fresh ideas to the system, and was very serious about improving students' performance, and teachers' morale. Mr. T reminded me of some of my experiences that I had shared with him on-going, in referencing visiting Western Countries, including Europe, as well as Eastern Countries, in Asia, and having lived in Singapore. He also knew of my involvement with various Community Organizations, and how effective throughout the years I had been with the students and parents. Mr. T insisted that I called Mr. Y to set up an appointment. It was because of previous experience with the "titled" individuals (males particular) I was very reluctant, and thus, told Mr. T that I did not feel comfortable in doing this, because I knew that there must have been a lot of people doing the same, with specific motives. During this time both were single.

Mr. T's persistence did not work. Therefore, he called Mr. Y to set up an appointment for me. Later, he called and communicated to me to expect a call from Mr. Y. Two days later, Mr. Y called and introduced himself. He related to me some of the conversation between Mr. T and himself. He was very pleasant on the telephone, and appeared to have been anxious to meet with me. During our brief conversation, a time was arranged for the meeting. Mr. Y asked if I would call his secretary to confirm the date and time.

After waiting for a couple of days, I received the standard confirmation letter confirming that everything was set. Meanwhile, I continued to chat with Mr. T, seeking any kind of information I could that would give me a better feel about Mr. Y. It had always been my practice to further acquire pertinent information about either the interviewer, and or the position advertised before the interview. Mr. T's behavior was somewhat evasive when I would ask him certain questions. Otherwise, he appeared

to have deliberately held something back. I felt a little ill at ease from the beginning, but carefully maintained my composure with Mr. T.

The date of the meeting had finally arrived. As usual, I dressed in business attire. I must mention that a principal had told me to be careful when I met with Mr. Y, because he had a sexual oriented reputation. I kept that in mind while carefully choosing the business attire. I considered everything she had said, and tried to make sure to prevent any kind of opening for a sexual invitation that would have obviously intervened with the purpose of the meeting with Mr. Y.

Upon entering into the headquarters, everyone was very polite, and demonstrated a sincere willingness to help visitors. A security guard caught the elevator with me, and escorted me to Mr. Y's reception area. I could not help but be impressed with all of the kindness that had been bestowed upon me since my arrival at the headquarters. It was a pleasant to have sat there waiting for Mr. Y, thinking of such kind behavior. Thus, this helped me to relax even more. After having waited for approximately 45 minutes, Mr. Y came out of his office, referring to me by my first name only, appearing to have acquired the "master" key to making one feel a part of, while not giving any kind of impression of one being a stranger, and or just an everyday professional. The first part of our conversation was about how the two of us knew Mr. T, and the respect that we both shared about him. It was apparent that Mr. T had shared with Mr. Y more than educational matters about me. Mr. Y knew about my National and International travels. He made reference to my having lived in Singapore, etc. I had given Mr. Y my packet that contained all the needed information. He very quickly glanced at it, appearing to have not been interested.

Finally, after our social encounter as mentioned, I politely intervened, and re-directed the on-going social conversation to a more business oriented dialogue. I began to share with him, some of my experiences, including educational workshops that I had done, both national and international, and some of the most impressive awards that I had received. At this point, Mr. Y started smiling. Being very naïve, I thought the smiles were an active feedback, signifying his appreciation for my having shown continuous activity and involvement to further help perpetuate the academic and intellectual growth for the educational community. I continued with that thought pattern, and Mr. Y paused and said, "why do you think that you are here?" That statement caught me somewhat off guard. My response was, "to share with you some of my qualifications, experiences and expertise so that perhaps you could find a position within the system that could best utilize my skills." I continued sharing with him and highlighting other experiences, that included comparing various educational concepts and strategies used with many countries and states that were making a difference with their educational systems. It was my hope during this dialogue, that he would take notes and began to do brainstorm with me on how some of these strategies could be applicable and implemented into our system.

Another interruption came, and again, he asked with a little more enthusiasm, "why do you really think that you are here?" At that time, while analyzing the tone of his voice, and observing his body language, I knew I had to answer this question with more affirmation. It was because of his actions, I was forced to react with a similar type of mannerism. I looked directly into his eyes, firmly and professionally, and responded by saying, "I don't know, why don't you tell me now?" The response obviously caught him somewhat off balance. He really did not expect for me to handle his comments in such manner. Nevertheless, he responded by making comments such as, "Mr. T sure knows how to pick them. I'll have to call my man, and commend him for setting this up." All I could envision at that time was "wow." Very quickly, I had to remember and analyze all of the clue words in that statement, without making any mistakes. It was no time for any type of behavior that would have either turned him on or off. After all, I had to forever keep thoughts of my future in mind with the system, as well as adhere to my morals and values.

As I sat, loss for words, because I was too overwhelmed to immediately respond to any part of his statement. I was thinking that I should leave immediately, because anything you say at this point could be detrimental to your hard earned profession. After a moment, I responded by asking him if he would review the information that I had submitted at his earliest convenient. Mr. Y did not respond.

I prepared to leave, he stood and started to pace slightly to and from his office door, while continuing to repeat, "he, (Mr. T) knows how to pick them." I shook his hand, and thanked him for his time, and left the premises. At that time, I was convinced that any probability of my having the opportunity to share any of my acquired with skills and knowledge, regardless to my experience would have been centered around SexCessFully doing so.

When I returned home, very annoyed, disappointed and stressed, I call Lady A to share with her what had happened during that meeting. Lady A had previously informed me as to what to expect from Mr. Y. She was very instrumental with helping me to cope with such a let down from Mr. Y. She also helped me to analyze and interpreted what Mr. Y's statement meant when he so explicitly asked those questions. I must admit that I already knew the answer to what Mr. Y meant by those expressions. Lady A said that if I had gone along with his behavior, I would have just become another one on his sexual list.

The Interview

Part Two

I recall having been sent on an interview to meet with one of the top executives by a very powerful and respected elected official. The reason for going on this interview was go become the Public Relations Director for the school system. My appointment had been confirmed and set for Friday, at 3:00 p.m. I arrived to his office approximately 2:30 p.m. When I arrived, there was no one else in the reception area. While sitting there, several men who were on his staff passed and spoke, and 100 percent of them exemplified the same expressions. Each asked if I were there to see this top executive, and thereafter, each had the sly grin on his face.

As I continued to sit, I read several periodicals like anyone would do while waiting for someone. Meanwhile, a couple came in, and appeared to have been parents, the time was 3:10 p.m. The executive's secretary finally came out and told the couple that they could go in. At this time, I re-checked with the receptionist to make sure that the time of my appointment was correct, although, I had a copy of the written confirmation in my hand. While continuing to maintain patience, the time now was 3:45 p.m. Another person came at approximately 4:00 p.m., and the secretary asked that person to go in with the executive. At this time, I was beginning to become a little suspicious of this so-called meeting. Approximately 4:30 p.m., the executive appeared in the waiting area, and said "I will be with you momentarily." Meanwhile, since the day was Friday afternoon, everyone was beginning to leave. It was time to call it quit for the week. As I continued to sit, one by one passed and said, "have a good weekend."

It was now 4:50 p.m. The telephones had stopped ringing, and the receptionist had packed up and left. The executive secretary also passed and with me a good weekend. It was now obvious that only the executive and I were left on that floor. Exactly 5:11 p.m., the executive came and asked if I would come into his office. As I got up from my seat, his eyes were locked from my waist down. Upon entering into his office, I politely asked where shall I sat? He quickly pulled two large chairs together, and asked if I would please have a set. He conveniently had arranged the chairs so that he would be able to engulf the total view of my anatomy. After he sat, he began to smile, very unusually. At one point, he realized how obvious the smiles became. Therefore, he placed one hand over his mouth, creating a bit of camouflage. While feeling somewhat uncomfortable, I began to speak. He did not address the purpose of my being there. My feeling of ill-at-ease became even more apparent, while trying to maintain my stamina. After all, I had already seen the layout of the floor, while having waited so long for the meeting. The area away from his office was very nice, and reminded me of the state-of-the-art hotel suite. It had everything that would have made one very comfortable, inclusively of a day bed, a very nice bathroom, with a walk-in-shower, love seat, regular sofa, a kitchen net, including a stove, refrigerator, microwave oven, a dining area with the nice high back chairs, and the décor was outstanding, excellent window treatment, flooring and coordinating pictures.

I continued to focus on the purpose of the real reason for this meeting, and that was the system needed a person with my skill and qualifications for a Public Relations Director. I noticed that his overt attitude showed that he was not interested in anything that I was saying. After having tried so effortlessly to adhere to the purpose of this interview, I was slowly getting turned off by his behavior. During my input, he would conveniently try to redirect my thinking into a social thought process. It was at this time, that I became even more convinced that this was not at all an interview, but an undercover proposition as to how far I would go. The type of body language would be used, either a "come to me look, or stay away from me look" could have implied which action would have been taken next.

As the time approached 6:30 p.m., I knew by now, there was only one thing left for me to do, and that was to somehow and professionally draw closure to that so-called interview. In my opinion, it was never intended to have been an interview for the Public Relations Director's Position. All I could imagine at that time was that if I would have prolonged my stay in his office, his intent would have been to try to make it a SexCessFully Promotion. Moreover, I packed my materials that I had brought to share with him and stood up. He appeared to have gone into a slight coma, not knowing if he had slipped or perhaps wondering why I was so naïve, and I did not pick up the "vibes" that this was never about an interview, but perhaps becoming a sex partner. As I began to leave, I extended my hand to shake his, and thanked him for his time.

As I walked to my car, I re-examined all of the behavior that had just taken place. I began to feel very frustrated, disappointed, and stressed. I knew at that very moment, that there would have not been any follow-up, or did I stand the slightest chance in getting the position. This was because my behavior was not acceptable to his demeanor. During the entire weekend, I fought very hard trying to overcome the horrifying feelings, while knowing that I had to return to the classroom on Monday, and having to keep silent about what happened on Friday, while continuing to perform all school duties.

Weeks had gone by, and there were no phone calls, no letter, or any kind of feedback from that meeting. However, I knew when I went for the position, that a Public Relations person was needed very badly. The school system was getting very negative publicity. It appeared that every day, news of some kind would infer that most significant others were either incompetent or just lazy. Also the media continued to report students in the system were performing at a much lower rate than its neighboring counterparts, thus, never reporting the many outstanding activities and achievements that were going on in the majority of the schools. Therefore, it was imperative that a qualified Public Relation person be put on board.

Many weeks went by, and still there had not been any communication from the executive. I was invited to a political banquet. The opportunity afforded me to be able to sit at a table with individuals who had just attended a social affair at one of the local universities. During our dialogue, an individual shared with me about some of the events and activities that were experienced. He shared some details about certain individual who were in attendance. Surprisingly, he said that the Public Relations Person from the school system had stood and introduced herself. I asked for more details, but he could not remember even her name, nor if she were currently work in the system. That conversation inspired me to the point, whereas I had the urge to further investigate, to find out more about her expertise, knowledge and experience that she either already had, or could have brought to such a failing system.

My feelings were that Lady C (I will call her) was not a part of the system, and further to make matters worse, I found that she was not a part of any public local school system. She was from another county. She did not have residence in the city, that once, I was told in order to get a promotion within the school system, that one must maintain residence in the city. I shared this information with the elected official who had set up my previous interview for the same position. Immediately he called her office and suggested that she contact me to learn what the school system was all about, and to have me to share the many excellent things that were going on in the system. It was his hope and desire to help her adequately prepare for such a vast task. She telephoned me, using a very unpleasant tone, and asked what could she do for me, and if she could help me in the future, to let her know. My response to her was that I did not particularly need any help from her.

After having checked Lady C's background, I knew that she did not know anything about the school system. Therefore, it would have been somewhat impossible for her to help me. Furthermore, it was she who needed my input and support. As I spent a moment thinking about the call, I began to wonder how could she had demonstrated such courage to have asked me something like that when people had been in the system for years, and had no clue as to the many excellent things that were happening.

Weeks went by. Before the 5:00 p.m. news came on, the promos indicated that there had been an incident in the system at one of the local schools. At the beginning of the news cast, the news focused on this incident as its headlines. As usual, when such information was being disseminated in reference to any of the schools, I stopped all activities, and focused on the broadcast. To my surprise, Lady C was speaking on behave of the school system. Lady c appeared to have been very uncomfortable, and she was totally unaffected in trying to tell the story. She had may pauses, and with many of the questions asked, she did not respond directly to the reporter. It was obvious by now that Lady C was incompetent, when was what in the "eyes" of some individuals attractive. Immediately, after the broadcast went off, I received several telephone calls from colleagues who commented on her responses. Some of the comments were that, where did she come from, and who had chosen her to speak for the system. I could not help but have flashbacks from the interview I had seeking the same position. I imagined how the executive must have approached her, his mannerism, his undercover proposition, etc., and because of that experience, I will always be curious as to what strategies were really used during her interview with him, and if this were a SexCessfully Promotion.

CHAPTER TWENTY-THREE

THE PITFALL

(Lost All Hope)

During this era in my career, I had sincerely tried many tactics to help to impact creative positive image of the school system. I had never given up on acquiring more skills. I continued attending workshops, spending my own personal money, paying for high price conferences, etc. It was because the trend in education had already moved into the technological era in essence, it was the computer age.

In the beginning, as I read about predictions in education as the 21st century approached, it appeared that the main focus was centered on computer and multimedia technology. I hardly knew anything, in reference to the concepts and principles about computers. Immediately, I went back to school to become familiar with this concept. I started with any introductory course in computers, and continued to take courses until I had accumulated 18 credits. Although, I knew the basic concepts about the computer, I did not become proficient with them until I purchased my home computer. While I was obtaining knowledge with this type of technology, the students remained my focus. I purchased various programs that were relevant to the subjects I taught. To no avail however, all of this became useless, because I did not have a computer in my classroom, as well as no compatible computers to my software within proximity that would have run my programs. All of the computers that I had seen in the school were Macs. All of my equipment and programs at home was IBM Compatible.

Again, I contacted some of the key players at headquarters to share with them the need for computers. I was not surprised when they could not relate to the importance of my request, and therefore, I was ignored. I did not stop there. I recall, after having heard many campaign speeches before election, how some of the candidates almost convinced me that once elected, their priority would be education. I contacted those individuals, and shared with them the pertinent need for computers in the classroom. Again, I was ignored. By now, I began to lose all hope. I had exhausted all of my connections. Therefore, my focus was on just doing the best that I could do, and with what I had to work with for the students. However, this attitude did not help make improvement in education. If one were to apply the more simple form of mathematics, and used subtractions, one would have realized that it has always been, nothing from nothing leaves nothing. In addition, one could use the expression, "GIGO", Garbage in, garbage out. Although, both analogies are synonymous, it does not delete the pain that a classroom teacher experience when working with children.

Just as I had become a little more relaxed, by having been convinced that I had exhausted all connections with individuals who could have made a difference, I experienced more unpleasant behavior that had taken placed in the school system. The following experiences will define this statement.

Experience Number One

(Ms. A and Mr. T)

It was approximately 6:00 p.m. on Friday afternoon, when I decided to try and relieve some of the built up week's stress, by having worked with outrageous overcrowded classes. I had concluded that taking long quiet rides away from the city helped to serve as a quick remedy. As I was doing my stress relief drive, I remembered passing a very secluded tavern like restaurant, that appeared to have been just sitting there all alone. I knew that I was in the county, but did not know the name of the town. After it seemed that I had driven too far, I decided to turn around, and re-track the route that I had come. I had not eaten dinner, and did not feel like cooking when I got home. Therefore, I consciously looked for that little tavern on the way back. As I approached the tavern, there were two automobiles on the very small parking lot. It never darned on me that this place could have been very dangerous for a female to stop. Before I made the final decision to stop, I viewed the entire surrounds very carefully.

I recall walking into the doorway, and there were three people at the counter. To my surprise, two of the people were Ms. A and Mr. T. Ms. A was a classroom teacher, and Mr. T was an executive from headquarters. I knew Ms. A from other social events. I had seen Mr. T at School Board Meetings. This place was a very small tavern, but sold food, and had the food list on a large board attached to the wall behind the sitting counter. There were no tables in the place. The only place to sit, was at the counter, that had a capacity for about seven people. Nonetheless, there were two seats between where I sat and Ms. A and Mr. T. Ms. A seemed to have been surprised an embarrassed when she saw me. She had been in the school system seven years. She was very attractive. Mr. T appeared to have been in his early 60's. I knew that he had been around for a long time. He did not show too much concern when he saw me. The place was very small, virtually empty, and there were no television or any kind of entertainment, it was very quiet.

After I sat and ordered food, Ms. A and Mr. T realized that I would be able to hear their conversation. At first, they did not talk for a while. I was smiling within, because it was not likely that they weren't together, and did not know each other. By the way, the automobiles on the parking lot belong to the two of them.

During their dialogue, they tried to speak, using codes. Unfortunately, Ms. A was so young, and did not understand what Mr. T was trying to do. Therefore, Mr. T had to somewhat "paint" the picture for Ms. A's perception level. After having listened to their brief conversation, it was obvious that they were making a deal. Shortly after, Ms. A was promoted from the classroom to headquarters. I would often times see Ms. A in the hall after having visited headquarters. Recall speaking to her, and asking her on one occasion, if she were visiting. She informed me that she worked there. I had to be very careful not to have shown any type of surprised behavior. I asked Ms. A what was her position. She shared with me that she had been placed in an executive's assistant position. After having seen Ms. A, it was no doubt, that I had just witnessed another SexCessFully Promotion.

Experience Number Two

(Ms. M and Mr. Y)

Under a new administration, Ms. M received a pink slip, stating that her position was no longer needed, and that the entire department that she worked would be dissolved after three months. Ms. M shared the thought of her having to return to the classroom was too devastating. She knew that conditions in the local schools had become progressively worst prior to her promotion. However, Ms. M had become very acquainted with Mr. Y, who was in a top decision-making position at headquarters. She shared with Mr. Y that she would beave education if she had to return to the classroom. Ms. M also shared that she knew about some of the unpleasant, and not advertised negative behavior that Mr. Y had done. Therefore, she expected Mr. Y to use his executive's influence, and help to find another position at headquarters for her.

Ms. M did not have any time to waste, because the termination of her department was very quickly approaching. Ms. M informed Mr. Y that she needed to have been secured in a position at headquarters before the end of the month. Mr. Y expressed to Ms. M that he would guarantee the she would not have to return to the classroom. However, Ms. M did not anticipate the price that she had to pay for the favor. Ms. M shared that Mr. Y called her at home, and informed her that he had found a position for her, and there would be no problem with making the transition very smoothly. In addition, Mr. Y shared with Ms. M that he was expecting a visit from one of his college friends during the upcoming weekend, and that he was in the process of securing the perfect date for him. Mr. Y informed Ms. M that he had concluded that she was the answer to his search. Ms. M was married, and would have been very difficult to have gone on a date with someone else on the weekend. Ms. M thought the date would have been an early evening dinner. She told Mr. Y that she would accept his request.

The weekend was nearing when Mr. Y telephoned Ms. M to inform her that his college friend was very excited to have been given this opportunity to meet her. During the conversation he asked Ms. M to bring an overnight bag to his house when she came to meet with him. Ms. M said that the news of having to bring an overnight bag could have only meant that she would have been the friend's sex partner. She recalled becoming almost hysterical, because she was too afraid to say no, as well as the consequences that she would have faced, if she said no. She knew that her career future was resting in Mr. Y's hand.

Ms. M's husband had made previous arrangement for the two of them to attend a social function on the same evening that Mr. Y had made arrangement for her to meet his friend. Ms. M shared that during the rest of the week, and because of the stress that she had accumulated, she became so ill until she had to receive medical attention. When she went to her private doctor, he admitted her into the hospital immediately. Ms. M did not share all of her symptoms with me. Therefore, when the time came for both appointments, Ms. M was in the hospital. She did not contact My Y, because she was ill.

After Ms. M was released from the hospital, and had been given permission to return to work, she shared that the first item on her agenda was to explain to Mr. Y what had happened. Mr. Y did not empathize with her. He expressed how angry he was with her for standing up his friend, and showing deception. After the brief dialogue between the two, a week later, Ms. M received a memo from with the bureaucracy that informed her to clean her present work area, and prepare for relocation. The relocation was not where Ms. M had anticipated. Ms. M had been demoted, and assigned back to a local school as a classroom teacher.

Ms. M could not have afforded to have quit her job, because of her financial situation. She adhered to the instructions from headquarters. After several months in the classroom, Ms. M noticed that something was somewhat out of the ordinary with her anatomy. She went to her private doctor for a complete checkup. The doctor informed her that she had terminal cancer. After the medical diagnosis of Ms. M's cancer, she became too ill to complete the school year. I recall, a year thereafter, I saw a colleague from Ms. M's school, and sadly was told that Ms. M has passed. The news of Ms. M's death was very traumatic for me, because I will always believe that her death was initiated because of sexual harassment.

Experience Number Three

(Ms. B and Mr. O)

Ms. B was a principal, assigned to a very troubled school that had been put on a list for immediate improvement. Mr. O was new, and in an executive's position at headquarters. During Ms. B's short tenure at the assigned school, and while serving in a principal's capacity, she made a vast difference in the total image and operation of the school. There was no longer exposure of severe disciplinarian problems, tests scores had improved, and more programs had been implemented. However, the school had made such a positive change, until, it was one of the few schools that the local media positively highlighted.

Meanwhile, the school system's history was the ongoing hiring of outsiders to make decisions for employees in the system. Moreover, the continuity in this case was not altered. A new executive was hired to clean house. I received a call from an elected official who shared Ms. B's story, as well as informed me that he had heard from Mr. B, who had informed him that she had not received a transfer notice, and the reason for the transfer was that she had been accused of being negligence and incompetent as the leader of the school. In addition, the letter stated that the staff and parents had requested her dismissal. Of course, none of the content of the letter was true. This was all created among individuals in key positions at headquarters who had another agenda for doing such. The other agenda derived as the result of a top executive at headquarters who had chosen a female (who had shared with the executive) to become the principal of this school. In return, the price for the promotion, the female was assigned to the executive's assistant to serve as his sex partner. After the female and the assistant had been together several times, the female made it known that she needed to have cashed in on the deal.

Ms. B received the communication from Mr. O within a week before the opening of schools for the next year. Ms. B seeked help from significant others, to no avail. Ms. B could not have contacted higher sources, because the higher sources held ownership of the executive.

Meanwhile, Ms. B exit, and the new lady entered. I must mention that, because of individuals in various positions, the news media had received very negative reports about Ms. B. The most puzzling about all of this, was that on one from society questioned the abrupt change. Needless to mention, the hard work to change the reputation of the school that Ms. B had done to bring about a positive image of the once very negatively labeled school. After having learned many stories as this, it was no miracle why I lost all hope and respect in the school system.

Experience Number Four

The Stalker

(Ms. D and Mr. C)

Before the expressing, "stalking" became popular, like in the 90's, individuals had been experience such continuously. Ms. D shared that after having a brief encounter with her principal, she was continuously threatened and stalked. By the way, Ms. D was an aid in the school system, and Mr. C was the principal of the school to which Ms. D had been assigned. Ms. D shared that in the beginning when she first started having sex with Mr. C, it was because she needed help financially. Because Ms. D was an aid at the school, her salary did not meet her basic financial needs. Therefore, Ms. D said that she knew that Mr. C was interested in her sexually. Her main agenda for consenting to become Mr. C's sex partner was to receive extra money.

Ms. D shared with Mr. C that he must give her money each time they had sex. Sometimes, Ms. D would contact Mr. C to have sex three to four times per week. Mr. C was married, with children, and Ms. D was a single parent. When Ms. D was sharing her story, she appeared to have been very pleased with her behavior. I recall two of the teachers from Ms. D's school sharing that the principal, Mr. C would have Ms. D spying on teachers, while they were in their classes. The teachers began to wonder, what had come over Ms. D. They noticed how Ms. D had made such a sudden change in her mannerism. She had converted from an aid, to an undercover boss, and or supervisor, so to speak. Ms. D began to really over-step her boundary when she would give orders to the teachers, using a threatening type undertone, and also informed them of consequences if the orders were violated.

The teaching staff began to suspect that something was not right about Ms. D's behavior. Meanwhile, several of the teachers had gone to the principal, and shared with him their dislikes in reference to Ms. D's behavior. The principal, Mr. C told them that he had not noticed a change in Ms. D's behavior, and that he did not appreciate them trying to create a problem in the school. Mr. C also told the teachers that Ms. D was a very hard and excellent worker, and that his plan was to keep her on the staff as long as he was the principal of the school.

At the next faculty meeting, without calling anyone's name, Mr. C informed the staff that he did not appreciate individuals on the staff who were trying to start trouble in the school. Very blatantly, he told the staff that he was not going to listen to any more complaints in reference to anyone on the staff. It was no secret, as to what Mr. C was referencing. Thereafter, instead of teachers reporting Ms. D's behavior to Mr. C, they began to retaliate on an individual basis against her. The teachers' behavior toward Ms. D created so much stress for her, until she informed Mr. C that she could no longer be his sex partner. This did not set very well with Mr. C. At first, he thought that Ms. D just needed a break. After a month passed, Ms. D had not been sexually involved with Mr. C. Therefore, Mr. C started following her after school hours. Ms. D said that early one morning during the school week, she happened to have looked out of her bathroom window, and saw Mr. C sitting in front of her house. Ms. D became very frightened, and at that moment, did not know what to do. One of her teenage daughters informed her that there was someone outside, and insisted to inquire about his visit. However, after about an hour, Mr.

C left, because it was getting close to the beginning of the school day. Ms. D was too afraid to go to school that day, and therefore called in sick.

Nonetheless, the stalking did not end with that episode. There were many other occasions that she would see Mr. C sitting in his car, and waiting for her. The most horrifying of all of the episodes was when Mr. C showed up at her church. After service, he told her he wanted to go someplace and talk. Ms. D had her children with her. She tried to explain to Mr. c that the timing was not appropriate. Thereafter, while at school, Mr. C evaded her presence. Finally, at the end of the school year, she received a pink slip from headquarters that informed her that she had been terminated from all duties in the school, because of poor performance and unsatisfactory rating. Needless to say, losing all hope and respect in the school system was inevitable, because of the many negative behaviors that individuals had, and were still experiencing in the school system for selfish reasons, while none of the behaviors were geared toward helping the students.

CHAPTER TWENTY-FOUR

THE CLEANSING PROCESS

(A Challenge to Move Forward)

Many years had passed, and I was still witnessing the same negative behaviors. These behaviors were SexCessFully Promotions, sexual harassment, fear, stress, while the students were failing even further behind n tests scores, as well as graduating each year, lacking in basic skills. Employers were speaking out in reference to these problems. Teachers were still the target, as well as other school based personnel. There was still no mentioning of the advertised behaviors aforementioned. Although, I had lost all hope in the operational and promotional processes within the school system, there were still children who were in need of help in many ways, more now than ever. The parents of the students were very young, and too often, they appeared to have been lacking in parenting skills. I recall one of my 12th graders, who mother was only 29 years old, had seven children, and no husband. Moreover, one may frown on that statement, but my average student was from a single parent home. Many of them were being reared by their grandmothers. They did not know too much about their grandfathers. In addition, many of the students only knew their fathers name, and in some instances, had never met them. Therefore, I knew that collectively, we all had to make a change, regardless to pass knowledge obtained.

It was sad having to talk with both male and female students, who had so much built up anger and pain, because of their environmental situations, inclusively. By having these types of experience with the students, and each year, it appeared that the students would have more problems. I decided that I was going to change my attitude about the school system's activities of which I was familiar. Therefore, deep within, I made a total commitment to helping the students and their parents.

Nevertheless, I had never stopped attending conferences and workshops, while keeping up with the current trends in education. However, in the past, I had done very little with the knowledge gained. I realized that I had been too hung up over dealing with the anger and other stress, and that I had allowed these intangibles to become obstacles, thus, prevented me from performance at my greatest potential. I began to seriously look at the purpose of the reason why I was a classroom teacher, and had remained in the classroom for all of those years. I have always believed that the Creator has everyone's life planned at conception. Too often, we tend to forget the concept, and try to overrule what has already been planned for us. With this sincere conviction, I began to feel much better about my not having been promoted. I felt even greater when I realized the strength I had, and the strength of keeping quiet, being able to sit at the same table with the sexual abusers, so to speak. The abuser represented individuals who had deliberately used every tactic to block justifiable promotions so that they could put a SexCessFully applicant in a position.

Moreover, I began to sincerely connect with the Creator. Although, during my entire life, I was never detached from the Creator, but from time to time, I did slip a little. The more I realized that there was a greater Power than top executives, elected officials, and school based administrators, the more excellent I became as a classroom teacher. Often times, it would surprise me of the creativity, innovation, and methods that were bestowed upon me to use with my students. These concepts most definitely had come from a Supreme source, because I did not know anyone in the school system with these types of skills.

During this era in my teaching career, there seemed to have been less resources, including both financial, materials, equipment and supplies. From the outcome of my students, often times, it appeared that all of these things were in place. I recall, as I would see my students progress by evidence of performance exhibition, I would experience less stress and anger. As a matter of fact, I was no longer angry with individuals in the school system. A lot of the same individuals were still in positions doing the same thing. I continued to hear about the same behavior. Instead of having become angry with the abusers, I would Pray that they would one day, become healed from their weakness.

It was very obvious for me to identify the individuals who were still being SexCessFullly Promoted. I recognized the characteristics very early in my career. Often times, I would mentally reviews the basic criteria. Some of these criteria were body size, light complexion (if African-American), the ability to dress very well, lacking of years in the school system, and lacking in skills and qualifications for the position. I would observe them struggling very hard in their positions, while trying to convince others that they belonged there. It was so sad to have observed those individuals. As I would observe their behavior, I would notice that they appeared to have been very unsure when trying to make presentations of any kind. Females appeared to have been experiencing a hormonal unbalance.

In my opinion, to have performed sexual activities to leave the classroom to become a principal was not good. However, most principals, regardless as to how they tried to shift the weight to classroom teachers were blamed for the students' failure. Therefore, unless the principal was given a "free-hand" from the high epsilon in power, often times the principals appeared to always be undergoing severe stress attacks, and in most cases tried to pass it on the classroom teachers. Moreover, as I observed the classroom teachers, especially those who had been in the system for a time, they appeared to have been immune to such principals' behavior. They would mention in passing about how they thought the principals had obtained the position. However, for most of the teacher, it did not matter. I never heard any teacher say or make reference to becoming a SexCessFully Principal.

Too often, the SexCessFully Promoted principal would always demonstrate such a negative attitude, as well as exemplify insecurity toward an individual who had the strength and courage to voice his/her opinion. It was always a fight between the principal and the individual. Like some of executives in key positions, this type of principal would use his/her title to try to keep individual suppressed who could have made a positive change in the school system. Very rarely, in a school would teachers disagree overtly with the principal, because of fear of receiving a poor evaluation, and or an administrative transfer. Many times, the principal was very unfair to the individual who was transferred administratively. Unfortunately, when most administratively transferred, teachers tried to share their side of the story, there was no one in position, who would listen to the teachers. Principals knew this, therefore, in many schools, teachers used the old cliché' this it was better to remain silent, and allow the principal to have his/her way, because in some cases, many of the principals were pathological liars.

Nonetheless, this attitude was very bad, because if the teacher and principal would work together, the outcome would have been growth in the students' academia. Both need to realize that in the business of education, there are disagreements in order to make a positive impact. There must be cohesive team work. I do not recall during my entire life, witnessing other types f businesses, whereby, all of the decision were made by the CEO. Therefore, if education was to change, I am convinced that the current practices of negativism must be overhauled, and allow the cleansing process to occur. The cleansing process will continue to be very difficult, as long as there are continuous SexCessFully Promotions, and or sexual harassment.

We all must have experienced during some part of our lives how difficult it was to function very positively, when we had the symptoms of illnesses, such as nausea, cramps, and migraine headaches. The outward appearance did not show any relationship between the illnesses. Therefore, if nature did not take care of these, often time we took medication to start the cleansing process within. Thus, this analogy demonstrates how we must think, if we are to make a positive impact with the children's education. In my opinion, it is my belief that an individual has the jurisdiction over his/her own behavior. One may choose to adapt to a very unpleasant behavior, or choose to fight through the bureaucracy to ensure the cleanliness of one's environment.

Finally, one must be strong, and believe in oneself. It should not matter about the rejection form letters after an interview, particularly, when one has met the qualifications for a position, and because he/she refuses to become sexually involved with someone in a key positon, one should not allow himself/herself to become engulfed with the uncleanliness behavior. One should stand firm on his/her beliefs, maintain his/her morals and values, and make the conscientious decision in reference to a promotion, whether he/she will walk into that position up-right, or slide into the position on his/her back.

CHAPTER TWENTY-FIVE

FREE AT LAST

(The Sigh of Relief)

In the words of Dr. Martin Luther King, Jr, "free at last, free at last, thank God Almighty I am free at last." During that era of my life, I never had the wildest dream that this expression would have directly affected me during my tenure in education. Although, not included in Dr. King's speech referenced that one day, all SexCessFully Promotions, and Sexual Harassment on the job would be abandoned from North to the South, East to the West, in the School House, at the Headquarters, in the City and State Government, in the Post Office, in Privately Owned businesses, and in other job markets. Nevertheless, because of my having to spend years witnessing SexCessFully Promotions, receiving rejection form letters, unfair treatments, and blocking positions by individuals in so-called powerful positions, all because I refused to drop my Spiritual Beliefs, as well as maintained my morals and values, thus, preventing myself to become sexually involved with those who pursued me throughout my career. In addition, many individuals did not receive promotions in their profession, because of the same reasons.

Even though, during the years, I suffered royally. I recall each time that I had to sit at the table with the sexual abusers, I always wanted to tell them the truth about how I felt about their practices. Like many others, I was too afraid of being reprimanded, or perhaps being dismissed from the school system. One in power could always write on paper excellent negative reasons for their behavior, particularly when it was always a one sided situation. Teachers were not allowed to express themselves openly and honestly. The most important thing about this type of hindrance was that it always appeared to society that because teachers had appeared to have been a part of a decision-making committee, then everything should have been all right, thus, providing a gateway for teachers' input. Not so true, what the public did not know, that often times, when teachers were chosen to participate on a committee, that it would depend on who was on the committee, whether a teacher was honest or not. Too often, teachers appear to have a built in mechanism that is stimulated, once around anyone with a title. Too often, the mechanism's composition includes: fear, low morale, non-appreciative, underpaid, not worthy, rejected from society, stress, burned out, and a large percentage of having to always take the blame for students' failure, as well as other negative connotations reflected upon education.

Therefore, it is no wonder, why SexCessFully Promotions and Sexual Harassment have always stayed alive, and maintained a very essential ingredient in the making of employment opportunities, and used as art of the criteria for the selection and decision-making strategies for securing a positon. However, is not that strange to anyone that these types of behaviors occur among employees and employers. The most unfortunate thing about all of this is that the average employee is too afraid to talk opening about each ingredient, because of having the fear that no one would believe him/her, and or the consequence of losing his/her job.

I recall a situation that occurred between Ms. C and Mr. X. Ms. C was promised that when she completed her doctorate, she would receive a promotion. Ms. C was a classroom teacher for many years. She had helped with many adverse situations in the school system, and the result of her effort was certainly noticed. Mr. X would recognize Ms. C's accomplishments publicly, sharing how pleased he was to have her as a staff member. Meanwhile, different individuals in decision-making positions continued to encourage Ms. C to complete her doctorate. Ms. C's physical characteristics were unlike a lot of the individuals who had been SexCessFully Promotions. Ms. C was in her mid 50's, appeared to have been about 5'0 in height, and weighed about 200 pounds. Although, Ms. C was overweight, she was very aggressive, and did not have any problem with facing different challenges, particularly if she thought that they would have enhanced her ability to help the students. Ms. C never appeared to have been excluded from the mainstream in society, because her name had appeared on various related schools programs. Ms. C continued to work very hard so that she could receive an executive position. The time had come for Ms. C to receive her doctorate. She was most deserving of her accomplishments.

After having received her doctorate, she contacted the individuals who had promised her that upon the completion of her doctorate, she would be promoted. Ms. C did not hesitate to forward her newly acquired documents to headquarters. She followed up with several telephones calls to key players. She did not receive any feedback, except that she was instructed to real all bulletins from headquarters that contained various job announcements. She followed the directions, and applied for an executive's position that would have caused her to relocate from a school based building to headquarters. Although, the position did not pay the salary for a person with her credentials, she added that she wanted it anyway.

Ms. C was never called for an interview, after waiting for over three months. The job description indicated that the position needed to have been filled immediately. Meanwhile, Ms. C became disgusted with her supporter. She began to search for other available opportunities outside the school system that could have best utilized her skills. Ms. C was fortunate during the job search to have been offered five different positions that were based on her qualifications.

Several weeks after Ms. C had taken one of the positions, her telephone rang in the afternoon while she was at home. It was Mr. T, an executive from headquarters. Mr. T informed her that the position that she had applied for had been filled, and asked if she would continue to apply for other positions as they become available. Ms. C said that she was more than honored to have experienced the Sigh of Relief, and become Free at Last from the school system. She informed Mr. T that she had accepted another position with a private business, and had received an executive's position that paid almost three times the school system's offer, as well as shared with him that she had become free at last, and had expelled the sigh of relief from education.

Nonetheless, this story was a good example of how one could become free at last, and experience a sigh of relief, but one cannot always change jobs, because of certain adverse conditions that are big factors in creating the need for the change. I believe that there is no perfect job. Therefore, there will be ongoing conditions that are unpleasant, this is to be expected. However, one does not expect to be sexually harassed or SexCessfully Promoted.

Moreover, there are many individuals who have done like Ms. C. Throughout the years, I recall hearing conversations in reference to the direct relationship of one's age and appearance in terms as to what position and promotion to expect. I believe that one's age and appearance should not play a major role in order for one to receive a promotion. In my opinion, this is the epitome of discrimination. I am aware that certain companies have dress codes. I do not have a problem in adhering to such. Nevertheless, I am concerned with wat society has defined as beauty, sexual appealing and attractive vs. qualifications and skills in reference to promotions.

I reflect back on the word, "inclusion," that played a big role in education in the 90's. I concur with the concept and principles of inclusion. I believe that all humans, regardless of their genetics should be give the same opportunity to be treated fairly, whether one is a student, parent, teacher, principal, executive, and or other. However, it is my belief that the same concepts and principles of inclusion should apply to all who are promoted, and should be based and skills and qualifications. It is my conviction that inclusion that is based on one's ability, yields very positive outcomes.

I believe that when individuals in a decision-making position understand the true definition of inclusion, and that SexCessFully Promotions will not be replicated and opportunities for all employees will be applicable.

I understand that it will take a strong committed person to adapt to this concept, because it requires a sincere commitment to education to be able to recognize others who work together to benefit the total educational process. When this happens, I am confident that all individuals will witness major renaissance in the school system.

Since I have come to the realization of how some individuals have operated within the school system, I no longer have to speculate projected outcome. The problem still exists, but if individuals would have enough courage and come forth, and report known SexCessFully Promotions and Sexual Harassment in their work place, I have enough faith that things will change.

I commend Ms. Oprah Winfrey for airing a program to help increase the awareness among females that made know that females had wings. This concept was made very clear by a television production that was entitled, "Before women Had Wings," and was based on an individual true experience. However, it is my belief that women have always had wings, but had not learned how to fly. On the other hand, women always knew the physiology of the wings, but because of fear and other obstacles, were too afraid to fly. Therefore, to relate to the relevance of this concept SexCessFully Promotions and Sexual Harassment among employees and employers, it is my opinion that women, and sometimes men should have enough courage to report this type of demeaning behavior. If there is no one in a top position who will listen, the next step should be seeking legal advice. There should not be any more reasons why one should have to undergo mine and others pass experiences, because of sexual harassment, as well as having to refuse to become SexCessFully Promoted, instead of being recognized because of one's qualifications. There should be no more terminal illnesses, or manic depressions syndromes affecting individuals, because of having been subjected to such behavior.

In addition, I am very pleased to have been experiencing freedom for the past five years. The freedom's origin was the result of creating a balance in my life. The balance was the result of my having started two businesses. Therefore, the opportunity afforded me to initiate justice and fairness among employees. It appears that each time that I do what is just, I experience more freedom and relief.

Finally, as I conclude this dialogue, it with a Sigh of Relief, that I have recognized, and currently, am free, although, the concrete pain of disgust and disappointment has been embedded into my subconscious, because of the many unpleasant experiences. I am truly pleased that I was strong enough to have prevented becoming SexCessFully Promoted, and also had the strength to have not allowed any of the symptoms from such to have interfered with my focus and performance exhibition forever.

Printed in the United States
By Bookmasters